Praise for Friends of Friends of Friends

Silver Medal in Relationships and Communication, Nautilus Awards, 2024
Silver Medal in Anthologies, Midwest Book Awards, 2024

"Reading this book and those incredibly insightful and personal thoughts, it feels like community works like stories in inoculating against the forces and moments that force us apart, helping us find our way back, or at least prove a companion until we can." Matt Foss, co-writer and producer of the award-winning short film, *Sons of Toledo* (2021), named one of the Austin Film Festival and Movie Maker Magazine's Top 25 Screenwriters to Watch for 2023.

"For anyone interested in exploring the role of community in supporting change, reducing a loneliness epidemic, or living a good life, there is a lot to chew on here." Dr. W. John Koolage, Professor of Philosophy, Eastern Michigan University

Praise for Death Never Dies

Gold Medal in Pop Culture, IPPY Awards, 2022
Silver Medal in Anthologies, Midwest Book Awards, 2022

"Despite the strange title, this is actually a compelling anthology of writings from a number of gifted authors, the majority without significant name recognition. The same can be said for the essay subjects. While you will find a tribute to Ruth Bader Ginsberg and Breonna Taylor, you will also find more than one name here that you do not recognize and wonder how you missed their lives. The various viewpoints provided thought provoking questions about the effect of their lives on society. This book is about legacy." Midwest Book Awards

Also by Robin Stock

Gridiron Glow-Up

The Opponent

Also by Lee Fearnside

Spark: Celebrities and Our Decisive Moments

Friends of Friends of Friends: Defining and Building Community

Death Never Dies:
Mourning 2020 through the Lives and Deaths of Public Figures

The Field Guide to Animal Adaptations

O! Relentless Death: Celebrities, Loss, and a Year of Mourning
(with Andrew Fearnside)

Letters to Our Children

Edited by
Robin Stock and Lee Fearnside

with essays and art by

Dorthe Alstrup
Hakim Bellamy
Caitlin Cacciatore
Ally Day
Maggie Denk-Leigh
Curtis A. Deeter
Deborah Haber
Holly Hey
Erin Holscher Almazan
Cynthia Katz
Michael Kocinski
D.S. Mohan
Sarah Rainey-Smithback
Michelle Otero
Sandra Rivers-Gill
Rachel Richardson
Janalee Stock

CHIMERA PROJECTS

Toledo, Ohio
2025

A Chimera Projects LLC Publication

www.ChimeraProjects.art

First Edition, October 2025

ISBN 978-1-7320964-8-6

Printed in Minneapolis, MN

Acknowledgments

I should first thank my co-editor, Lee, for her willingness to work with me on this idea. I said, "I want to work on something creative," and she has been an amazing mentor and partner through this process. Thanks also to my husband, Jesse, who has always been supportive of the hours and hours of sequestered time it takes to bring written projects to life. My parents have long been cheerleaders of my writing. They buy and read my books, even the ones they're not supposed to know I wrote. And finally, of course, I should thank my kids—Alia and London. They were the inspiration for this idea.

Robin Stock

Robin, thank you for being a great collaborator and being up for doing all the things. I appreciate all of the contributors' trust in us. I especially want to thank all of the people who helped me see myself as a parent, including my own mother and father. They demonstrated that parenting, creativity and independence could co-exist. Holly, thank you for being the best co-parent, especially when I didn't know what I was doing (the shushing!). This is for Oscar, who is my heart outside of my body.

Lee Fearnside

Contents

Dear Reader:

I don't quite remember how old they were. Young, for certain—still in elementary school and more than four full years apart. I don't remember which car I was driving or the weather or where exactly we were going to eat. I do, however, remember that my son and my daughter were in the back seat, and we were on our way to eat dinner, just the three of us. My husband might have been overseas on his second year-long deployment to Afghanistan, but he could have just as easily been tied up at work or playing soccer or on a long bike ride.

Those details, to be truthful, are irrelevant because here is what I do remember: We were driving down the big hill on Cable Lane, and one of the kids used a swear word. The other giggled and I was about to give a half-hearted scolding, but instead, I made a game of it.

"Okay, let's do the alphabet. Tell me every swear word you know for each letter, starting with A."

"Asshole!" a tiny voice blurted from the back seat.

"Asshat!," the other followed.

Then it was bitch and bastard and buttnugget. I put the kibosh on the C word before anyone could say it, but dickhead and dingleberry and douchecanoe were all on the safe list. And honestly, many (most?) parents would have been terribly concerned that their elementary-aged children knew so many swear words, but what I remember is the breath-stealing, wheezing laughter that came out of all three of us. My daughter, the elder of the two, knew the most words, of course. My son, still only in maybe first or second grade, hardly knew any, but with each new word, he devolved into a fit of giggles so infectious that I can still hear the sound in my mind today, now more than a decade later.

My kids remember it, too. They are now twenty-two and eighteen and they still talk about the time Mom let them say every single curse word they knew. In Pixar terms, it's a core memory. It will be with them forever and as a result, I don't regret it one bit, because it taught them that they can have a voice, that they can choose what power words have, and that a little humor goes a long way.

This is important, because there are other moments—big moments—where I didn't get it right. I must live with the unending guilt of those mistakes forever. I have had to say "I'm sorry" a good number of times, sometimes in situations where "I'm sorry" wasn't nearly going to cover it. Sometimes, in the worst moments—where mother and child might as well have been from different planets—I wrote to them. I would write to them to remind them that I loved them. That I thought they were talented and charismatic and capable and intelligent. I reminded them of all the things I knew were true about them. Because, ultimately, being right in an argument was less important than reminding them that they were loved. Unconditionally, truly loved. I wanted them to know that I wanted them, that their lives meant something—especially to me.

As we worked on this book, there were so many relatable moments. Moments of guilt. Moments of anxiety and worry and frustration. Moments of pride and want and joy and failure. Missed moments and moments found in unexpected places. No matter the age, the number of children (including the choice not to bring a child into this crazy world we live in), the cultural background or whatever other difference, it was impossible not to connect with these stories in very real ways.

In some ways, this book has a bit of an Alpha and Omega feel—not in a spiritual way, but in the way it explores themes of birth and death and everything before and after and in between. At the beginning, there are questions. The first: Is parenting for me? Should I bring a child into the world? And then: Oh my god, how do I keep this thing alive? Am I doing this right? And after that: Please don't let me make the same mistakes my parents made.

In some ways, our first entry, *Elegy for an Empty Womb*, is both Alpha and Omega. It is a poetic lamentation on the environmental state of our world, a love letter to a child who will never be. Caitlin Cacciatore's gut-punch of an essay is both beautiful and painful as it opines the reasons she will never subject a child—even a child she wants—to a future so environmentally unstable.

Throughout the book, these works explore the gritty reality of life through lenses that are at times joyful and at others remorseful. The very real effects of mental health and addiction are present in several of these works. In *Jess*, Janalee Stock writes to her eldest son on his fifty-first birthday. In unflinching style, she tells him she was ill-equipped to be a mother at nineteen. She was a hippie, living in poverty in Appalachia, desiring of men and parties and alcohol—a lifestyle that drove her to a suicide attempt, even as she was working to finish nursing school, working to give them both a better life.

In *A Letter to Theo*, Curtis Deeter writes to his son in congratulations on the eve of the birth of his first child. He uses humor to connect the reader to the relationship and bond between father and son, and his tone stays light throughout the piece, even as he lays out a volatile childhood and, eventually, the suicide of his own father. He shares that many moves during his young life made it hard for him to create bonds with others, but in that ever-jovial tone, advises his son not to shut people out.

The essay *Letter to My Children*, by Michael Kocinski, uses journal entries as windows into young parenting. He refers to his children by their birth months and he writes about the "black dog." The black dog, which might be depression or existential dread or anger or any other number of maladies destined to drag a person down. And he offers hope in a way that feels both direct and real, but also lyrical and lilting like a lullaby our weary minds didn't realize we needed.

And *Every Part of this Letter is About Love*, by Sandra Rivers-Gill, is the story of a Black mother, always there to advocate for and uplift her children. She writes, "But parenting is not for the weak," as she shows, time and time again, the strength required to be the mother her children most needed. She writes about the decisions mothers have to make, the moments they decide that they must confront that coach or that teacher on behalf of their children, who are often afraid to speak up for themselves.

Our final entry explores death—the true Omega, if you will. Deborah Haber's *Letter to Zeta* is a painful reminder that we can, unfairly, outlive our children, despite our most noble efforts to love them in full, imperfect color. Deborah writes, "I used to have conviction," but that losing her child to suicide has shaken her to the roots, has left her with "a lifetime of Wednesdays."

In today's society, we see parents judged—often quite publicly—for their choices. Complete strangers act as judge and jury in response to single moments in time, often behind the veil of online anonymity. It takes bravery to put ourselves out there, to tell our stories even when we know that we will be judged for them, no matter our intentions. I don't know if I have the courage to write the stories I should. The stories that say, "I'm sorry for not handling that life-changing situation the right way." The stories that say, "I cannot live without you. Please value your own life as much as I do."

Like many others, I usually only put the good stuff out on social media. I don't post about the ways in which I've messed up, or the challenges I am facing, or the crippling anxiety I feel every time my kids walk out the door. I am supposed to be the strong one, the organized one, the one who holds everyone else together. I'm certainly not going to admit to failure on a public forum, where people I don't know can judge me and tell me all the ways in which I'm messing up my kids. No thanks, I'm not brave enough for any of that. But the authors featured in this book? They are.

As you read these essays and view the accompanying visual art as a reflection on parenting in another form, we hope you will be moved by their honesty. These are diverse voices, all facing their own challenges and joys while managing generational trauma, personal demons, financial and emotional stress, and all of the other "life stuff" that creates the quilt of life with which we will all, eventually, be buried.

We hope you will observe and offer grace. This book is about the complicated feelings we have for our children. It is about the choices we make for them, about the ways we change because of them. It is about our hopes and dreams for who they will become, our pride and worry and satisfaction for who they have become. It is about making choices, in some cases, not to have them at all and it is also about the unthinkable possibility of losing them altogether. It is about advocating and fighting and remembering.

This is not your mother's parenting book.

These are *Letters to Our Children.*

Robin Stock
August, 2025

Elegy for an Empty Womb

For M.

the disembodied voice of the child I'll never have
echoes through the cathedral of my mind. she is
humming a song that has not yet been written. I
gave her a name, but then I buried it in my oceans,
and it hasn't surfaced since. I mourn her, but

she is better off in a realm beyond existence,
safer, yes, in the recesses of my mind, where
she can hide in a dusty broom closet and seek
all the knowledge of every book I've ever read.

sometimes, she'll lament I never learned
the names of the Muses, or the saints, or
any of the Gods she'd rather be praying to.

there is no shame in holding onto something
precious, not even when you hold on so tight
that it flees from you, like a bird set free.
sometimes, you have to love the idea
of someone enough to let them go.

Dear Mariana,

I apologize for trapping you in the amber of moments unlived, but you must know one thing about the woman who never laid gentle hands over a belly swollen with child: I love you enough to let you go.

I often lament that I was not born in an earlier time. Part of me feels like an antiquity, a relic of another time aging poorly, like brass that tarnishes or steel that rusts. I am a product of another time. I write long, rambling poems. I seal my letters with wax. I would rather someone call me than text me. I am someone who my generation left in the dust as they soared to the stratospheric heights of climbing the corporate ladder and dreams of corner offices and promotions, marriage, and eventually parenthood, but I cannot join in their revelry.

I am a woman scorned, and hell hath no fury like the fires that rage inside of me, nor can the Biblical hell of yore hold a candle to the widespread ecological disruption and anthropogenic climate change that is here and is yet to come.

Mariana, I cannot bring you into this burning world. When I face my Gods in the afterlife and am asked about my role in the slow death of this world, the only planet in the universe known to harbor life, I will fall to my knees and admit to my guilt. Yes, I was complicit. No, I didn't do enough to stop it. But I loved my only daughter enough not to drag her soul through the same suffering that will befall others of her generation.

Sometimes I imagine you growing inside of me. Tiny fists slowly forming fingers. Cells dividing and doubling. Your exponential growth from zygote to fetus; your soft features. In my mind, you look much like I did, as an infant, which was identical to the way your grandmother looked as an infant. If one photo weren't in black and white, the other in color; you might think we were the same child from different angles.

I am a carbon copy of my mother. I look like her in almost every way, having inherited little from my father save for a long genealogy of nobility. I have my mother's eyes. My mother's face. My mother's smile.

Looking back at pictures of your grandmother as a woman slightly older than I am now, I am often struck by the similarities in my own visage. It is like looking through a mirror into a stark version of the self I will become.

Mariana, I named you after the deepest trench of the darkest sea. You take your name from the lowest point in this world, because I buried you deep inside of me and I promise I won't ever let you out. Are you not safer inside of me? Your unborn potential, slowly petering out like a candle that burns low. One day, sooner rather than later, my period of fertility will have run itself dry and I will be as barren as all the worlds hanging lifelessly in the sky.

I will never touch your face, nor wipe your tears. I won't ever wash a scrape or kiss a boo-boo better. You are the part of me that I am willing to sacrifice, because I love you, despite your absence. I love the idea of you, and an idea you shall remain, because life isn't fair, and we live in a time of great turmoil and rapid change.

I read in a book on ecology that even if carbon emissions were to stop today, the warming of this world would continue unabated for a thousand years.

And how, Mariana, could I subject you to that? How could I bear you, knowing you will face sweltering summers, rising sea levels, blizzards that pile dozens of feet of snow atop cars and houses and trees, hurricanes that grow more frequent, damaging, and deadly each year? One recent year, we ran out of the English alphabet and used up most of the Greek one too. I'm not sure there is a protocol for which alphabet to use after that. I have put forth the suggestion of the Phoenician alphabet–but I am glad that you won't live to find out.

You are my child, born or unborn. My only wishes for you, daughter, are for you to be safe, happy, and free, and the world we are headed towards will grant you none of the grace your great-grandmother took for granted, none of the freedoms your grandmother enjoyed, and none of the opportunities I have been able to take advantage of.

This world is unsafe for you. Scientists predict that the place where I am sitting right now—at the IKEA desk I assembled myself—will be underwater in fifty years' time.

You are far too precious to me. I cannot allow you to witness the scramble for northern territories, the exodus from the coasts, the climate change refugees numbering in the millions.

These are just some of the reasons I am on a birth strike.

Mariana, if ever in that liminal space between existence and imagination you wonder why I won't free you from the dark oblivion of my womb, it's because I love you more than you will ever know.

I love you enough to keep you safe from the ravages of time. I love you enough to keep your memory alive despite the life I never gave you.

There is nothing else I can do, Mariana. I am complicit in the slow, inevitable extinction of untold thousands of species year after year.

There is so much I could teach you, like how to find the moon through a telescope on a clear, cloudless summer night, or where Orion is and which star is Betelgeuse and you'd marvel that something so bright that burns with such fury – could die, and how it would take hundreds of years before we saw the supernova, even if it were to happen today.

You would grasp at the vastness of space and you would push against the punishing pace of time: always trying to find more of it, to save it, to spend it wisely, as though it were just another currency—like dollars or drachma—instead of seeing it as what it truly is: your life, slowly unfurling.

Except, like a flower that fails to bloom, your life is halted before its start. You never were able to reach the starting line, let alone the finish. It's not your fault, Mariana, nor is it mine.

Oil barons robbed me of you. Men with guns stole you in the dark of the night, long before I was even born. The last of the white rhinoceroses will not perish during your lifetime, because 'life' and 'time' are both concepts you ill understand, your shape and form torn between vastness and void.

I wish I could sit with you while you struggled over fractions. Maybe you'd get to go to prom, some time in an amorphous future that will never exist for me or you or anyone. Your would-be partner will go with someone else, always wondering where their missing half went. I will never get the pleasure of seeing you graduate from high school nor walk across a stage to be handed your college diploma. I won't be cheering in the stands at your soccer practice or track meets, and I'll never have to discipline you.

I'll never have to break the news to you that your dog passed away overnight, or how that means she's never coming back. I won't scold you, nor praise you. I'll never lift you in my arms, not for a first time nor a last.

There will be no one to care for me in my old age, but I'll always carry you in the places within me that are bereft because of your absence. I'll always keep you—like a treasure—sunk at the bottom of my well. You are my crowning jewel.

You'll never tarnish nor lose your luster. Age will never weary you, and time will only tell if I will be condemned for your loss, or rather the losses of the world because you will not be in it.

In the eyes of the oil baron, you are just another casualty of the war against mother earth.

But in my eyes, I am beholden to you, my daughter, and if I could gaze upon your face, it would be like looking through a mirror into my own past. You'd have your mother's features, and from your donor, you'd have eyes so blue that people would have gotten lost in them.

I'll never hold you when your heart gets broken, because your heart—your small, invisible, unbeating heart—was never broken. Yours is a magic land, beyond time. You exist as a state of potential. You are the daughter I wanted but could not bear to have.

We were supposed to leave this world a better place than we found it.

Mariana, you mustn't be swayed by these words; 'I apologize' is just another way of saying someone is sorry they got caught. But you have my deepest regret that I could not bring you into this world because of the sins of my forebearers. It isn't enough, I know, to say that I tried. I signed petitions. I studied up on recycling. I put metals and plastics and glass in their appropriate receptacles and threatened your grandmother with Amit the Devourer when she did not do the same.

I don't know if this is true, but they say that in the afterlife, your soul is to be weighed and measured against the feather of an ibis.

I am burdened by the weight of my crimes. The atrocities that my generation perpetuated against the natural world. It sometimes makes it hard to sleep at night, the weight of it sitting atop my chest like the monster you knew all along was under your bed.

I will be found guilty—but you. You are still pure and perfect, tucked away in your dimension where all dreams go to spawn, like salmon being propelled down a river at great speeds into the estuary where they will go to lay their eggs.

I wanted to name you like they named the stars in days of old, but once it became clear to me that you were never to arrive, always and forever lost in that never-land of youthful fairytales and storybook fables, I named you after the abyss – for that is where you'll remain, safe in the deepest trenches of my memory, secure in the darkness of my womb, sleeping so soundly that light does not reach you, or if it does – it is only a faint echo that does not rouse you.

I love you, Mariana, as much as any mother can love their child, and more—I love you enough to let your soul fly free in plains far from here and now, eons away from this place of suffering and storms and rising, raging seas.

Where you are, it is calm. The sea is silent. Deep and dark, it cradles you. My womb readies itself for your arrival each month, and every time, I remind myself that sometimes loving someone means letting them go.

Yours always,

Your Almost-Mother

Caitlin Cacciatore

One day if you're rifling through my boxes and find a plastic baggie protecting a little stick with two lines, don't touch the stick because I peed on it.

I had struggled with the inconceivable concept that I might be incapable of conceiving. Every month brought a new round of disappointment and an indication that my body was an enemy of the dreams of my mind. When I finally looked down at the two lines daring me to believe, I felt sick in the best way possible—trembling, churning, a fountain bubbling with joy, fear and disbelief. Did I take the test wrong? Did I misunderstand how to read the lines? Maybe two lines meant not pregnant? Would I be the one percent who received an inaccurate result?

Before you were born, I was the grown-up that all the kids loved. A silly storyteller who loved to fold to the floor to read, make-believe, and create. I dreamed, prayed, and begged to carry this over to my own children one day, confidently believing I would be the perfect parent, who explained things rationally and patiently, with humor and eloquence, so we'd live in eternal harmony and familial bliss.

Go ahead. Have a good laugh.

Welcome to parenting: The crash call to an all-consuming job, of the utmost importance, with absolutely zero training. We pass judgement on those we deem ineffective, until we realize we are equally clueless when our ideals swirl down the drain, replaced by a paralyzing fear that unleashes wave after wave after wave of worry. We are constantly analyzing, second-guessing, and re-assessing, unsure of finding footing in the mudslides of the once self-assured mind. Never knowing if you've done the right thing, consistently unsure of the choices you've made and the boundaries you've placed, incessant self-scrutiny, rattles the psyche. Was this the battlefield to anchor my flag on? Did I do the right thing? Why is parenting so frustrating? Am I just bad at it?

It's hard to believe you and I were once one, as you grew in the safety of my womb. I stopped caffeine, chocolate, shellfish, and everything else that the doctors told pregnant women not to consume at that time. In my mind I had the control to keep you safe and healthy, and I didn't care what beast of craving had to be tamed. The mere thought of you gave me an energy that carried me through the fatigue and morning sickness, as I obsessively read everything related to pregnancy. I was driven to be the best me to help you flourish.

All hands on belly, your dad and I would sit around in otherworldly intoxication with the goofiest grins, imagining who you'd look like, places we wanted to take you, and what you'd grow up to be. We talked about which traits we hoped were passed on to you, and which ones we really hoped were not. Buoyed by celestial clouds even as my girth grew, you made my toes tingle with a joy I'd never experienced, even after I couldn't see them anymore. And yet, even then worry hid like salt in ocean air. Is there something more I should be doing? Are peanuts okay or not? Would a defect take you from me before your first breath broke through the barrier?

The day you were born, at first sight, they placed my heart into my arms. Nothing compares. The intensity of our love and the immensity of caring for another being, gave your dad and I the deer-in-the-headlights look, yet simultaneously, we marveled at your magnificence and basked in your blessing. Tiny toes, tiny fingers—that nose, that yawn—the sweetness of your scent, the snuggle of your skin... unconditional love and pride swallowed us whole. In those moments pure joy and ethereal bliss blasted any appearance of darkness. But always lurking, the tormenter, partnered with tiredness, and launched into tsunamis of sanctimony: Are you getting enough milk? Is poop supposed to look that way? I might cut you if I cut your fingernail, but you'll scratch yourself if I don't cut your nails.

Dreams and dangers kept me awake, as I clung to the hope of maintaining some semblance of control: breastfeeding through the pain of mastitis, sprinting my tired body in the middle of the night from my bed to yours, so I didn't worry we'd roll over you in our bed, and swaying until I couldn't feel my feet.

And it continued: Washing germ-filled dirt down the drain in the baby bathtub, slathering sunscreen on skin and topping your wild hair with a wide-brimmed hat, optimizing organic options, safety seatbelts and security steps all in the name of trying to protect you from any storm.

The inner mother bear padded through packing endless snacks perfect for little fingers fumbling with fine motor skills, digging in the dirt so you'd know where food came from and how to nourish your body naturally, listening to a song or reading a book of your choosing for the millionth time, even as the words were fingernails on a chalkboard to my mind, or answering your questions with uncompromising honesty like why we didn't buy useless capitalistic consumer-centric crap, in the middle of a meltdown.

Even good things were tinged with fear. After trips to the library, I wondered if we were reading enough of a variety of books. After travels and museum adventures, I wondered if we were overscheduling. A once, mostly-self-confident woman, I found endless ways to question my parenting. Should I cover the left out Playdough or let you learn on your own? Should I give into your pleading to tie your shoe instead of letting you struggle to master it on your own? Was that kid on the playground playing too rough?

Comparison was a thief from the beginning. It started with milestones. Were you rolling over, sitting up, eating solids, and walking in time? How about throwing a ball and getting the ball in a hoop? Should I be nurturing your talent and find you a coach or let you continue to explore all the sports? Was I holding back the next Tiger Woods or Serena Williams?

As you grew, a new set of concerns grew, especially as you started school and experienced a life separate from ours. Would this be the last time you'd think I knew everything, the last kiss in front of your classmates, or our last bedtime story cuddled together. Fast forward through the teenage years of "my parents don't know anything, even if they think they know everything," the "you don't need to know everything, I can take care of myself," and the overwhelming dread of possibly receiving that one life-altering call from which there is no return. My heart ached for those mothers who received tragic news in a world filled with shootings and accidents that seem preventable but aren't prevented.

For so long, every morning with my coffee, I swallowed the sickening possibility that this could be the last time your eyes would meet mine, the last time our hearts would beat in rhythm, the last morning I kissed you and said, "I love you."

No matter how hard I scrambled to create a perfect world for you, there were always more obstacles in the way. Soul-crushing, hide in the house, and lock all the doors feelings overwhelmed me. Was it safe to let you go to the sleepover? Was the person driving the carpool looking at their phone when driving? Was your friend group pushing you to do things before you were ready?

In my mind, anything I did never seemed like enough, but I couldn't stop. I wouldn't stop, because you deserved more. You deserved everything in my power to give. From peals of laughter from the park swing, snuggling sighs under the blanket to watch a movie, to oohs and aahs filled with wonder and amazement exploring new places together, you kept me going and prevented me from becoming a prisoner of those monsters.

At times maybe it felt like I was fiercely over-protective as if I was trying to mold you into a little me. In my defense, all I can say is this was my first time. I was growing with each of you. I offered what I knew, what my experience had given me, as a foundation from which to build your own experiences and understandings. I tried to center my parenting around health, safety, love, information, and most importantly, the ability to think for yourself, but I was limited by what I knew and everything I didn't.

There were times that I disappointed you, where I failed, or I failed you. My "shoulds" were mistakes wrapped in my history. "You should study. You should find something better to do with your time. You should find someone better to spend your time with." I didn't always handle those situations the best way. There have been times where I've clung to the regret, berating myself for it. But being your parent helped me recognize that we don't stop trying just because we've failed. We learn acceptance or we'll remain frozen, unable to move forward, unable to be the best we can be. For you I reframed my thoughts. I handled those situations to the best of my ability in that moment.

You might think there have been times when you disappointed me. Maybe you saw me tilt my head back during a game where you missed the pass. Or I scolded when you didn't do well on a test because you didn't study. Or you overheard me grousing with my friends. None of those things were disappointments. Am I proud of the things you've accomplished? Yes! Do I love you more because of them? No. You are loved in totality, not because you are perfect, but because you made my life more fulfilling with your presence and filled me with an inexplicable love that I never knew I was capable of.

As teenagers we all fear becoming our parents. It's the given rule of teenage angst to rage against all things parent. That was certainly me. With time, and becoming a parent, I came to see things from my parents' perspective. And how their experiences guided their love. I hope you will see I did the best I could with every ounce of love I had to give. I know no one can be your everything, but you all come close. How blessed we are.

Now when I look back, it was pointless to yell about staying out too late, or nag about your messy room. Were those opportunities I missed to create another memory with you? It all boils down to I cannot go back and right the wrongs, and honestly, I wouldn't, knowing how proud I am of who you are today. Happiness, anger, frustration, triumph, helplessness, each emotion brought us to here, because we didn't allow fear to paralyze action.

I thought my love would save you, when in fact, my love for you, saved me. You showed me that everything will be all right, that whatever I was doing was enough, even when it didn't seem to be enough. I doubted whether any of things I did, made enough of a difference. You helped me see, showing up and living my life to the best of my ability, was enough as I muddled through motherhood despite the inability to save you from cruel comments, horrifying ignorance, or pervasive prejudice.

Parenting is a twenty-four/seven job that doesn't leave time for adulation so I'm going to take this moment to pat myself on the back, for whatever part I played that helped you become the wonderful person you are today. I didn't throw in the towel (even when it was wet with all sorts of fluids). I didn't parent occasionally, or silently from a distance. Good or bad I showed up every day. I did my best in the moment, with the information I had. I was not living my life for you. I was living the life I was meant to live for me, with the bonus of being your mom. Ultimately, the lesson I hope you take away was that I wasn't perfect and there are many things to fear, but I strived to be the person I wanted to be for you.

But my love clearly had limitations. I couldn't shelter you from the tears of friendships turning cold after a sleepover where you wouldn't go along with the crowd, the loss of innocence when a teacher unjustly punished you for standing up to a bully for hurting your friend, or the sickening cruelties of the world toward our fellow human beings. But I hope you keep in the back of your mind, what the world can be, not what it sometimes is. As the world feels ever more uncertain in a constant state of shifting like sand at the will of the ocean, I hope I've taught you, you need not be anything more than you are right now. In any moment when you are questioning purpose, duty, and future, give yourself the grace to know you are doing all you can in this moment and that is enough. Remove yourself from the equation when everything isn't adding up-read, get out in nature, listen to music, but the most important thing is to return when you are ready. Any setbacks or shortcomings you see, can be mitigated with faith in everything you have inside. Often doing something, a step in any direction, when fear tries to engulf you, is better than doing nothing.

Most people are hard enough on themselves. But often, so convinced their way is the right way, other people will judge and try to hold you back. Don't let them. When college rejections lead you to doubt yourself, when your love for another is not returned, when you don't get the job you wanted, you might internalize the loss and hold yourself back. Try not to. Your dad and I believe in everything you are and have been. Like the Legos you built, broke, and rebuilt (that we sometimes found under our feet at inopportune moments), build, explore, and create through the journey in front of you, for that journey is life. The one thing that burns true in your life is you. When things turn dark, I hope you'll see you are the light. This life is yours. Live it your way.

Surround yourself with people who believe in you and approach life with inner strength. The friends who help you laugh, relax, and hope. The burden of this world is not yours alone to bear. Look back and appreciate how far you've come, because at times it is too easy to fall into the mental trap of only looking ahead and becoming overwhelmed. From pulling yourself up with the help of the sofa and waddling to the kitchen to open every cabinet, to walking into your first day of school, and in a blink of an eye walking across that graduation stage, every little step got you here. Every little step will get you there, wherever there is.

There will be bends like elbows and knees, peaks and valleys on a long and winding road. The path is never direct. There is no, "if I do A and B, then C will happen" in life. So open the D for door even if it falls between A and B. Change. Grow. Believe in yourself. Make the difficult choices and be assured that you made the best choice in that moment with the information you had. We all know no one is perfect. But we approach perfection when we strive for living the life we've been blessed with.

Fill your life with gratitude, perseverance, and peace whenever possible, for life is precious. Your dad and I were forever changed when we lost your grandfathers. Any blame, anger, and regret, seemed incredibly insignificant in the face of losing a parent. I think we somehow felt we were always justifying our actions or trying to prove something to our parents. I'm here to tell you, you have nothing to prove to yours. You are a gift of infinite possibilities that you share with everyone who is lucky enough to know you. Treasure the random smiles and unexpected joys, store them in a safe place until you need them. The human mind is unfathomable. When I look back, many of the difficult times are lost in the haze and dust of time. I see memories that make me smile, they anchor my soul and fill my heart with delight of a time long gone, in the precious, peaceful appreciation of hindsight. I'm so glad I clicked the seemingly endless parade of pictures that drove you crazy sometimes. The memories they captured light up synapses in my mind like firecrackers.

As our family's favorite band, Coldplay sings in All My Love, "we've been through high, every corner of the sky and still we're holding on together." Are there any magic words that I can write to help you hold on? I don't know which ones really matter. But that doesn't stop me. No way to know how long I'll be with you. But in those moments when you feel alone and are shattered and sore, I hope and pray you'll recognize the strength within, to face the unknown with an open mind, trusting yourself, speaking up for yourself, and moving toward your beliefs, regardless of what's happening around you. I'll be there, because no matter how far we are, we are tied closer than we realize. An oasis of love rests for you in our memories and in our hearts. The moment you came into this world a legend was born. Even if there is nothing beyond and we aren't in the heavens watching you below, the beauty of this moment with you is enough, because you are enough. I wouldn't change a thing.

There is a quote from Henry David Thoreau on our refrigerator, "Go confidently in the direction of your dreams. Live the life you have imagined." I have lived the life I imagined and what a gift you have been in it. Carry on, never letting the naysayers stop you from rising, again and again. Journey with purpose, staying true to yourself, with integrity and honor. Show up, like you always have, knowing our love is eternal.

Jess

The picture sat above the stove in our Meigs County home. Maybe it was one of the Mother's Day projects a teacher would have her students do every year. Your hands had been dipped in paint and pressed onto an extra-large colored paper, just above a big hill. A happy scene, endeared with a smiling sun, trees and colorful flowers. The words "Make the most of everyday, for life does not stand still, someday these hands will wave goodbye while crossing life's brave hill" jumped out at me.

The details of what grade, teacher, escape me. Were the words typed out and pasted on, or did you write them? And most of all, whatever happened to this picture I treasured? Too many moves, too much chaos in the early years. It is gone, but the message remains firmly planted in my core. Unlike that happy scene, it was messy getting there.

I gave birth to you at nineteen years old, five years prior to me getting sober. I loved being pregnant. The first subtle flicker of movements brought joy, followed by clues you might become a soccer player. Those kicks at the ribs became mighty. I attended exactly one Lamaze class. Everyone had partners and your biological father had left town only weeks beforehand, never to be seen again. I brought a guy friend to that class but it felt too awkward for such an intimate experience. I didn't want him thinking about my "private parts." I was painfully aware my circumstances were vastly different from the other couples who were knitted together in a promising future. Their blanket was security, mine was a crazy quilt.

I read a birthing book instead and practiced the breathing techniques on my own, determined to have a natural childbirth. How hard could it really be given women had been doing this since the dawn of man? I did a fair amount of reading about how to have a healthy pregnancy. One suggestion had me drinking nutritional yeast in my orange juice everyday while holding my nose. I quit smoking, but there was one thing I couldn't quit. I was delighted to learn beer is loaded with B vitamins, but for someone on the road to alcoholism, if one is good, several are even better.

I was ill prepared for motherhood. I had left home at seventeen after dropping out of high school. I was just getting by, living paycheck to paycheck. I was still very much in the sowing wild oats stage of my life. "Immature" would be the apropos term, but in my mind I was something out of a Jack Kerouac novel. I wanted the fireworks, the full tilt boogie of living right on the edge. I was a junkie for chasing highs, whether that was in a mushroom, a new lover, or the independence of thumbing a ride. I wanted freedom with a capital F.

Just hours after I gave birth to you, I marveled. It was the highest I had ever been with no drugs involved and, being a junkie for the buzz, came the thought "I want to do that again!" I brought you home to a house shared with two other women, both Ohio University students. There was no baby car seat, no bassinet, just a dresser drawer stuffed with blankets to cradle. It didn't matter, I preferred to keep you at my side through the night, easier for nursing and I was not married to the clock when it came to feeding. I followed your lead.

When you were just a couple days old, I recall walking up Lancaster Street to what used to be the Welfare Office to apply for Aid to Dependent Children. Cars were expelling fumes into your beautiful, pink, perfect lungs. Horrified, I draped the blanket over your head and decided I would take a less traveled route next visit. There was that fierce need to protect you, but it competed with a desire to get loose, and sometimes the drink won as the weeks went by.

The reality of our situation bore down on me with time. I didn't want to be on welfare, nor could I hope for more than a fast food job without a high school diploma. My part time job modeling for art students paid well but was not going to lead to a nine to five. The solution came out of savoring your birth. I would become a midwife, so I could be present while babies were born and thus experience that ecstatic moment of a new life over and over again without having to have twenty-five children. It would provide a living wage and home births were in the demand back then. I just needed to buckle down and get responsible, although that word still made me cringe.

I passed my GED and was going to nursing school by the time you were a year old. I made the necessary external changes to try to look the part. The ring came out of my nose, a bra was donned and I was no longer wearing patched jeans. We had been living on a remote farm where we had to dip a bucket down a well for our water. It had two fireplaces, and the kerosene lamps created a cozy glow at night. It was an idyllic time, so much art was created, great books devoured, and woods explored with you tucked in a backpack. As much as I loved that home, I decided with school starting it would be more practical to move to town. The internal changes came harder. I had a strong work ethic but I rewarded myself often by going to the corner carry out and buying a quart of beer as I returned home from classes.

Making these changes and going to nursing school was more of a brave hill to be crossed for me than you. You didn't seem to have any separation anxiety, even starting preschool. On my end, the thought of embarking on a career that included giving shots, inserting catheters, and asking, "did you move your bowels today?" made me nervous.

You were an exceedingly happy child through those years, making friends with people I didn't even know. We spent lots of time on Ohio University's college green. You'd run around pretending you were the superhero from your favorite TV show. Since a four-syllable word comes hard to a two-and-a-half year old, it took me a while to catch on as you pulled your t-shirt off, shouting "Incredible Hulk!" I was just "Jesse's mom" to the people you befriended. You were the social butterfly, meeting and greeting people wherever you went. Maybe a bit of Grandpa Stock was passed on to you in that way. I had to chuckle when, as an adult, your family would call you the "mayor." You naturally saw all people as potential friends from the get go.

I have wondered if you and I just got lucky with your personality, given the first few years of your life. We didn't have much, save a dream of getting off welfare and finding a real home, a more settled life. None of this seemed to phase you. You adapted to circumstances without pause. Could it just be wishful hoping on my part? I remember one day doing laundry with you at the Ambassador. Another patron made comments about how amazing you were, helping Mama like an adult would, transferring clothes from washer to dryer, trying to fold clothes neatly into piles. Perhaps you were forced to grow up fast because I was on the slow-to-grow, Peter Pan plan.

Juggling nursing school and a part time job as a nurse aide was not easy but there was a cadre of women friends with children who relied on each other frequently. My weekend job at the hospital began at 7:00 a.m., so rather than drag you out of bed at 6:30 a.m. to go to the babysitter, you'd spend the previous night at the babysitter's. I would take advantage of those kidless nights and go out to the bars until the wee hours of the night, often arriving to my shift hung over.

My second summer in nursing school we moved into the three-room log cabin built by my friend Carol's great-great grandfather deep in a hollow. Rent was cheap. Carol was also going to nursing school and her daughter Jessie was your same age. Carol called her Blue Jay while we lived there to cut down on confusion, and despite no running water or electricity yet again, things went fairly smooth. There was a mule to plow the garden and chickens that nested in a fruit tree each night. We used the creek to keep food cold and lit the fireplace on chilly mornings. The real challenge was looking the part on hospital days with my pink striped pinafore, over a white uniform. I almost didn't pass my clinicals that quarter, with my smudged shoes and wrinkled attire frowned upon. My nursing instructor sat me down for a serious discussion about my appearance. My inner child tomboy had to concede; I was entering a profession where white caps were still pinned to the head, and as soon as the doctor arrived on the floor it was expected you would give up your chair immediately. Roles were well defined, and boats were not to be rocked.

Subsequently we moved from the cabin to a farmhouse, renting a room from my sister's ex husband. Would that make him an ex-uncle then? Another close friend of mine, Sandy, also lived there. It was ideal as her daughter, Chloe, was already your best buddy. There was still plenty of partying to be had, but electricity and plumbing made things far more manageable for the last quarters of school.

My big hope was that with nursing school done in 1978, we would just leave town, start over. As I finished up all my classes I weighed thirty pounds more than I do today, and it was all beer weight. I realized from my nutrition studies that I was getting all my Recommended Daily Allowance (RDA) in calories with my almost-daily twelve-pack of beer. I switched to the Light brand but the math still didn't compute, nor was it just the weight that was troubling me.

After you went to bed, I would go out drinking. I promised myself frequently I'd stay home but the call of missing out on a potential prince charming loomed louder. Guilt, shame and remorse became my regular bedfellows as I woke up occasionally to strangers. Blackouts occurred. I knew something was wrong with me but the very nature of alcoholism translates to an inability to see the truth. I could wake up in the morning, sick to my stomach, hands shaking, and shudder at the antics of the previous night, but within an hour or two the need to drink would lead to a different deluded lens - "I was the life of the party" or "can't wait for Friday's party."

I am thankful it is a life you barely remember. I loved you deeply but I was remiss in making your well-being my top priority. I am deeply sorry for that.

The truth began to dawn on me that summer after graduation. The real problem wasn't Athens, or other people. It was me. The thought that you would be better off without me circled my mind daily. I caught myself weeping in front of you just like my father did when he was drunk. That helpless feeling of having the caregiving roles reversed crushed me as a teen. I didn't want that to happen to you. One day after filling Uncle Harry's truck with gas, I broke down crying when I returned to the cab with people staring. The look on your face told me I was repeating history. The only reason I was driving Harry's truck and not my car was because I kept having fender benders when driving under the influence. The insanity and selfishness of my thinking was apparent. At that moment I crept another inch closer to the decision.

Well, you know what happened.

I don't think you actually remember when things came to a head on September 5, 1978. It was an incredibly beautiful morning. I could see that with my eyes but I could not feel even one iota of awe. This just further compounded a feeling of utter hopelessness. When Sandy got home from taking you and Chloe to the park I had already downed a six-pack of beer and a bottle of aspirin. A second one followed when I heard her car pull in. There was also the razor blade. The scene became a blur, as the buzzing in my ears (a symptom of salicylate poisoning) mounted by the minute. It was not a "go quietly into the dark night" attempt, but rather a disastrous scene with a lot of blood, as I was wrestled onto a gurney by a sheriff and EMTs.

There wasn't a "brave hill" for me or even a wave goodbye that day, and my failure as a mother was not absolved by surviving that attempt. I shudder when people say, "I didn't have the guts to do it" regarding suicidal ideation. What takes guts is asking for help. Eventually I did, and I am grateful I got a second chance at this life. I don't know that I will ever be able to truly make up for the hurts I caused, but it has been a worthy goal.You asked me once after many years sober if I couldn't indulge in a beer with you at a restaurant, saying, "It was so long ago, Mom." That told me perhaps you remember very little of where my drinking took me and for that I am most thankful. The answer was—and remains—an easy, "No, I can't take that chance."

It wasn't for lack of loving you, that I tried to check out, it was just a lack of imagination. I couldn't see any way out of the rut of my own thinking. I didn't really want to die, I just felt there was no answer to what ailed me. It's hard to understand how anyone can do the unthinkable, how they can cause so much agonizing pain to family and friends. Only someone gravely depressed or impulsive can think the act of suicide will make life better for loved ones.

Thankfully the story doesn't end there. It was a long time ago now. Forty-six years of continuous sobriety and working a whole lot on the "inside job" has made "make the most of every day" my life story ever since, and yours too.

Fast forward to the fine young man you became. We went through a few more rough spots as the years whizzed by, but your self-confidence, strong work ethic, and boundless energy kept you rock solid. Running, fishing, Dungeons and Dragons, and mountain-biking kept life fun through those teen years.

Like me, you grew restless towards the end of high school. I shouldn't have been shocked when you came home one day and announced you had signed up for the Army, but it was never on my radar for your future. Taking you up to the bus depot in Athens when you left for boot camp was hard. You at the window, waving goodbye as my heart revolted and the bus pulled out. Getting that phone call from an infirmary bed, you terribly sick from a combo of the flu and drills in the Georgia heat pulled my heartstrings taut. Years later, saying goodbye before each tour in Afghanistan was even harder. I knew your days were long and stressful, yet those FaceTime phone calls with your kids from your sleeping bag in the wee hours of the morning were golden and reflected a commitment that defied fatigue and fears.

"Make the most of every day." You have embodied this in so many ways. The "contract" you and your wife outlined regarding what you each needed for a healthy relationship was such a revelation to me—so mature! Your intentional dates to ensure your marriage stays vibrant are also to be admired. You are the fun factor when the cousins get together. "Let's grab the bull by the horns" is in your DNA. Your sense of wrong and right, and integrity, comes with a big dose of both passion and restraint. You are committed to giving your children opportunities you didn't have. Coaching soccer, all of your jobs doing good service for communities, there is no shortage of ways you make me proud. You have a full life, and it's just one of the many things that give me a big dose of happiness when I think of you.

And now you have turned the corner at fifty-one years old. Why do numbers sound so weird? What automatic meaning do we attach to them? Still, I just can't believe it...somewhere in my head and heart you are all the ages all at once.

Because life does not stand still. This second is the past, in one second. The wave goodbye begins really at birth. The first time the nurse put you in the bassinet, halfway across the room at the hospital, I thought, "No, we were one unit for nine months, you can't just take him away from me and put him in that hard plastic box!" And then over and over again, we get practice—off to a babysitter, preschool, college, the driver's license of life that demands we go out into the world and claim our own space, our own path. I've enjoyed watching you cross that brave hill. You are a ray of sun in a world that needs light. The painting you brought home in elementary school speaks to me in every way as I reflect on a cup that has runneth over on your birthday.

Even at the final goodbye I know I will be thanking the universe for the gift of your life. Continue to Carpe Diem! We have crossed many brave hills both together and apart, and there are still more to come.

Grateful beyond ordinary words.

Love,

Mom

Janalee Stock

I desire to hold, to hold onto, to grasp and struggle to let go. I am at a point in my life where I am myself, but do not feel like myself; in which my sons are increasingly pulling away from me and finding their own voices and their independence. This is all at once wonderful and heartbreaking. This body of work navigates this emotional space of attachment and detachment, of holding and letting go, through the use of color and with an emphasis on hands and touch.

Erin Holscher Almazan

Adam Sleeping, oil on paper, 40" x 26", 2025

Slow Down, oil on paper mounted on plywood, 15" x 15", 2025

Wild Boys, oil, graphite and cold wax medium on paper mounted on board, 30" x 22", 2016

DIVA™ Cups and China

Dear Oscar,

You were about two years old and walking, but not steadily, while being raised by two moms living on a rural route in a flat, fly-over state. Our family benefitted from industrial agriculture's impact on our organic garden. Cicadas would sing us to sleep, and our Bichon Frisés (Tricky and Thurlow) would wake us up, barking loudly at the neighbors' target practice with their AR-15s. For a two-year old you could pronounce Tricky and Thurlow very clearly, and you could also say Mommy and Mom-Mom as clear as day, as well as short phrases and sentences. You were also very good at repeating back what Mommy and I would say to you.

I was in my mid-forties during your toddler times and being pounded by peri-menopause. I didn't understand what was happening to me. No one was talking about it, like Oprah or Ellen, or maybe I missed these adult conversations because we were watching *Dragon Tales* and *Wild Kratts* and going to sleep soon after you. My sleep was often interrupted by hot flashes and anxiety. Most days my brain floated on a thick, dense fog that reminded me of the low-lying moisture that would crawl across the humid summer ground. I was exhausted all the time, and my body hurt all the time. I was filled with rage, and I didn't know why, and I told myself that I didn't give a shit. But I really did give a shit because that wasn't really me, and I really didn't want you to ever experience my rage.

I was at the point in my life where my menstrual flow could not be contained by mere tampon or pad alone, or by combining pads and tampons, or even by combining tampons and tampons and pads. I needed a level of protection down there that I never fathomed in my younger years. I don't remember how or when I discovered the DIVA™ cup, but using one bolstered a new confidence for me throughout those days and nights. Inserting and removing the cup was fairly easy but required a decent range of motion, a yoga-type flexibility, a little deep breathing, as well as some mindfulness about my posture.

In those days, I often awoke in a reactive arthritic state when menstruating, inflammation everywhere in my body, fatigued, and experiencing general malaise. My stiff joints and swollen tissue limited my range of motion, making it painful to twist enough to wipe my butt, much less deal with the DIVA™. I remember one morning when I tried to remove the cup, my arm wouldn't stretch forward and down to take it out. When I couldn't get to it when sitting, I stood up and tried, but my range of motion was even more limited and the pain more intense.

I cried out to Mommy, "Sweetie, the cup is stuck" and "I need your help."

I slowly sat back down. When Mommy arrived, Tricky and Thurlow were on her heels and greeted me on the toilet. I told Mommy to get the dogs out of the room. She did, and then she suggested that I stand up so she could grab the cup from the front side of my body. I put my hands on her shoulders, squatted a little bit as she put one hand on my shoulder, while she reached in with her other, grabbing the cup and pulling down, but it would not budge. She moved behind me. I put my hands against the wall and squatted down a little deeper this time. Mommy tried again and failed. I returned to the toilet and then suggested that we move into the playroom where I could lay down on an air mattress that doubled as your bouncy bed.

Mommy and I moved into the playroom. Tricky and Thurlow followed us. I asked Mommy to get them out and keep you at bay in front the TV or something. I didn't want the sight of my blood to scare you. Mommy shooed the dogs out and left the room to tend to you. When she returned, she shut the door but not all the way. It wasn't long before you lost interest in what you were doing or being alone and came to find us. You pushed the door open, toddled in with the dogs behind you and sniffing at the breakfast smoothie in your sippy cup. Eventually, they turned their attention towards me, laying half naked on the bed. Both jumped up and began sniffing around. Mommy shouted, "Get your snouts outta there." You walked over and said, " Down doggies, down."

They did not obey any of us as I attempted to explain to you that I had a small rubber cup in my vagina that collected blood from my period, which was perfectly normal, and that Mommy was going to help me remove the cup from my vagina because I could not grab ahold of it because I was sick. By this point, Mommy was laughing really hard, and soon you started to laugh really, really hard. You also started to stomp your feet, turn in circles, and race around the room while gleefully shouting, "Mommy take cup from Mom Mom's China! Mommy take cup from Mom Mom's China!"

Eventually, Mommy got a good grip. The suction released. The cup was out. Mommy departed quickly towards the toilet with the DIVA™ cup in hand and the dogs on her heels. You and I were still laughing. Before I could pull up my pants, you ran super fast towards me and threw your little body against the bouncy bed. Your sippy cup exploded and splattered all over the lower half of my naked body.

I cried out, "Sweetie, I need your help," and the dogs came running back in.

Holly Hey

A Letter to Theo

Dear Theo,

If you're reading this, that means you're about to become "Dad," too. Mazel tov, kid. Things are about to get interesting. Before they do, I have something I need to say to you:

I'm so damn proud of the man you've become. Seriously.

I wasn't always dad of the year. I tried. Believe me, I tried. But in you, I see versions of myself I either never found or found too late, and every day I'm more and more impressed. In you, son, I see that I did my job better than I ever imagined.

It wasn't an easy job. Not for anything you did, but for all the things I didn't know. The list is embarrassingly long, and can I tell you a secret? Promise not to tell? Okay, here it goes:

I still know absolutely nothing.

Which reminds me of a joke you used to play. It went a little like this:

"What's your name?"

I'd respond with "Dad" or "Curtis" or "Aloysius Leap." The latter to get a response from you, to move you closer to the punchline.

"What's this?" you'd ask, pointing to your nose that's also your mother's nose.

"Nose," I'd say. Or "booger cave" when I was feeling "extra."

"And what's this?" you'd ask, holding your hands out.

I'd scratch my head and shrug my shoulders, try to come up with a clever way to delay the inevitable, like saying, "Your hands, of course." Or, "Just air, right?" No matter how many dumb guesses I offered, you'd always get me in the end. It was nothing. You were holding nothing in those hands. With that cleared up, you'd hit me with the punchline, a mischievous grin on your little face.

"What's your name?"

"What's this?"

"And what's this?"

The answer? Daddy. Nose. Nothing. Daddy knows nothing.

You'd laugh and look to your mom or Grammy or Grandma B.B. for comedic support. Your eyes would light up as I shook my head and sighed. You got me again, for the fifteenth time that afternoon.

There're two lessons in this story:

Number one, never think you have all the answers. You don't.

Number two, whenever your kid involves you in something, be it a "stupid" joke or a story you've heard a googolplex times, a game that doesn't make any sense and has no rules until you break them, or a storm of emotions you can't possibly understand, participate. They came to you for a reason. Be there. At the end of the day, that's all you can do.

Before we get started, I'll teach you a third lesson for free. Remember when I told you being a parent isn't an easy job? Well, it's not easy for your partner, either. Never forget that. On days when you're upset over a petty slight, whenever you feel like rolling your eyes or screaming, remember. Just like you, they're doing their best. They're giving it everything they've got. Somedays, that's more than others. As cliché as it sounds, you're in it together. It can never be you against each other. It's always you, together, against whatever road bumps come across your path.

And trust me, kid, there will be a lot of road bumps. Some small, some big. Some you'll see coming from a mile away and still hit at fifty miles per hour, bottoming out so hard you'll think you're about to break down. Others will catch you by surprise. You'll be cruisin' along, enjoying the scenery, well on your way to whatever destination you choose, and bam! Everything will come crashing down.

You'll miss out on a promotion or opportunity you've worked hard for.

You'll grind to reach a goal, and one day, you'll grind too hard. It'll feel like everything's coming apart (remember when I thought I was Mr. Strong Dad and blew out my shoulder? Yeah, that's the kind of thing I'm talking about here).

You'll lose someone (if you haven't already, and chances you haven't aren't great, unfortunately), and it will be so unexpected, so devastating that it will forever change the way you view life and death.

All these awful, jarring bumps in the road are here to tell you one thing, and one thing only. Our fourth lesson:

Slow. Down.

Life is both fast and long. Don't blink too much, and don't wait until it's too late.

I want to tell you a story. As your mom has pointed out on so many occasions, I tend to ramble. This one won't be an exception, but the lesson at the end is worth seeing it through. Hey, there's number five, and I wasn't even trying to be wise this time:

The important things in life take time and effort. Anything easy to come by probably isn't all it's cracked out to be.

Anyhow, here we go. You may have heard bits and pieces of this before, but I've never told you the whole story.

My dad, your Grandpa Bobby (who would've loved you every ounce as much as Grandpa Dan, Grampy, Papaw, and Dzia Dzia), was an alcoholic who battled depression (something I've fought my entire life, and if I've passed it along to you, I hope we're at a place in our relationship where you know you can always come to me with any problems you have). He was, of course, much more than the booze and his mental health issues. He was a police officer, a lover of animals, and a poet. Most importantly, he was a father, something every man I've ever known has yearned to be.

What I remember are happy, seemingly insignificant moments like playing Mickey Mouse on his computer; watching Oscar the silver dollar fish swim laps around his fish tank, dodging bubbles as they rose from the filter in the corner; planting a cherry tree in the backyard, wearing one of Grandpa Bobby's T-shirts down to my knees. He was my dad, and when I struggle with losing him so early in my life, I try to remember him as that and only that.

Eventually, Grandma B.B. and Grandpa Bobby got a divorce. When Grandpa he could no longer be a dad, when alcohol and depression got the better of him and he lost everything, he couldn't see a way back. Then, when I was four, my dad died.

After two more men called "Dad," Grandma B.B. and I moved, but I can't tell you that story. It's not mine to tell. What I can tell you is that packing up your life and leaving everything behind sucks. I did it not once, not twice, but three times. From Missouri to Wisconsin, Wisconsin to Illinois, Illinois to Ohio, with a lot of extra stops in between. Changing area codes started to feel as common as changing my underwear.

While moving only a state away might not seem like a great distance, when you're young, and your friends are all you've got, a state away might as well be Mars. This was before cell phones and social media and whatever kind of crazy communication devices we have now, and when you no longer lived next door or didn't ride on the same bus, it was only a matter of time before you became strangers. When so many friends become so many strangers, you start to ask, "What the hell is even the point?" You stop trying to make friends, because you know you're going to lose them as soon as they get close.

But try not to feel that way. Teach your kids to cherish every moment, every connection, no matter how fleeting they may seem. Each piece you pick up along the way shapes who you are. Even the blank ones.

I held onto anger for a long time. Anger, in some ways, is easier than joy. It gives you an excuse to blame others. Let it go. Whatever it is, it's not worth it.

When Grandma B.B. told me the truth about Grandpa Bobby, after years of letting me believe that he died from a disease like cancer or a bad case of the flu, my anger became rage. Why would my dad kill himself? Hadn't I been enough? And how could she lie to me for so long? These were my parents. I was supposed to be able to trust them. They were supposed to take care of me, and here they were, one abandoning me, the other lying to my face. I was so mad, and I didn't know how to handle the emotions surging through me.

At first, it started as small rebellions: buying and wearing chain parachute pants with zippers (so embarrassing. Thanks, Grandma, for "accidentally" throwing them away); piercing my ear with a safety pin in the bathroom at school; forgetting to turn in my homework.

Small rebellions turned into close calls: getting caught stealing candy from the teacher's lounge; being "held back" in math because I failed to do the work; falling downstairs and nearly breaking my face on concrete. It's impossible to say how many times I did something stupid, yet the consequences (or lack thereof) weren't anywhere near proportionate. Someone was looking out for me, even if I didn't think I was worth looking out for (Grandpa Bobby? God?).

Whoever it was, I know they're looking out for you, too. Just like I always will, kid.

Because I was so angry at the world and never learned to take responsibility for my own actions, I turned to anything I could find that could ease the weight of responsibility. Video games, cigarettes, alcohol, weed. Harder stuff on more occasions than I'd like to admit. As you know, I gave all that stuff up as soon as I got my head out of my you-know-what, but not before facing real, life-changing consequences.

I lost a lot of great friends; I disappointed my family so many times I lost count; and after a traumatic and terrifying experience involving police and guns (theirs, not mine), I spent time in jail, albeit much less time than I probably deserved (again, thank you Grandpa Bobby, or God, or whoever was watching out for me).

I learned how to let go of anger and resentment (mostly), how to live with the same depression and doubt your Grandpa Bobby must have faced, and why it's foolish to rely on external forces to dictate your path in life. I grew up. I became a better version of myself, someone who was worthy of being your father. Lesson by lesson, I made a life for myself so I could make a better life for you and your mother.

I was never sure if I was enough. There were always doubts. Do I really deserve any of these blessings?

Until now. Until I look at you and see the man you've become. A kind man. A funny man. An important man, who, like in one of the first books I ever read you, has succeeded. You have, indeed (98 and 3/4 percent guaranteed).

Why do I tell you all of this? Well, because I need you to know. You only get one me, and I want you to understand that even though I act tough and seem like "Super Dad," I'm only human. A better human because of you, but human, nonetheless.

And so are you.

You're going to make mistakes. You're going to say things you regret. You're going to yell when you later realize you should have offered comfort, compassion, and patience.

There are going to be days when you are more afraid than you've ever been. So afraid you'll lose sleep, and it will be hard to eat without feeling sick to your stomach.

An example (one of many):

When you were small enough to fit in my hand, you had a high fever we just couldn't seem to break. We Googled your symptoms. Big mistake. If it's still a thing, never, ever Google your symptoms! We found there was no other possibility. You were clearly dying. If we didn't get you to the hospital immediately, we were failures as parents.

At the hospital, they ran innumerable tests, and each new negative result sent me pacing faster and biting my nails lower. If it wasn't strep, then what? If not pneumonia, what horrible rare disease could you be inflicted with?

"The only thing we haven't ruled out is meningitis," a young, ambitious E.R. nurse told us. "We have to do a spinal tap, or it could damage your son's brain forever."

"What, it could? Okay. Do it. Do it, now!" we said, sleep-deprived, hungry, desperate.

Just thinking about it makes my blood boil. But remember, we're letting go of those kinds of emotions. I'm forgiving those doctors, here and now.

It ended up being a common cold, by the way, but I can't begin to describe how scared we were. Sorry to say, you'll learn soon enough.

There will also be days when you're so lonely it hurts. You're going to have friends who become strangers, and it's going to seem like you'll never make friends again (you will). Meeting new people is freaking hard when you're an adult and all you care about is your family. Not everyone will understand why you're obsessed with being Dad. Or Husband.

Like we said, anything worth having is hard, but one morning, you'll wake up and realize you already have it all.

Not only is parenting not easy, but life isn't easy. While I'm writing this, I can't possibly guess what path you've taken, but you got there. And that's the hardest part. That alone is worth celebrating.

So, cut yourself some slack. You're not always going to be perfect. You're not going to make the right decisions when everyone is looking to you for answers. You can't always be the best version of yourself (that's when you need to remember how amazing your partner is!), and that's okay. Do you know why? Because you are you, and you've already won. You're exactly where you need to be, and guess what? All those terrifying things you have no idea how to handle? You'll figure them out. I promise.

I've lost track of how many I've shared, and maybe you've found some I didn't even mean to include, but I have one last lesson for you. More a request, really:

Never stop playing. There was a time in my life when I forgot how to play. Then, I met your mother, and life slowly started to become fun again. Anytime it stopped feeling fun, I reminded myself to keep playing, to stop taking everything so damn seriously.

When you came along, I finally realized what life was all about. What could possibly be more fun than being a dad? To be honest, I'm a little jealous. You get the rare and beautiful blessing of experiencing fatherhood for the first time. Buckle up, kid. It's going to be so unlike anything else you've ever experienced.

But if you're half as good a dad as you are a son, you're going to be amazing. Here's to you, kid. I can't wait to take this next step with you.

Sincerely,

Dad

Curtis A. Deeter

Every Part of This Letter is About Love

—To my children

We met in the belly of our beginning. I swaddled you in black tapestry—the language of our ancestral experience; who we are, weaved into a vibrant quilt of our record; our artistic fabric handed down, to cover you like God's grace in the space of your choosing. I knew the world's accommodation would try to rapture you in its meagre means.

I had your back long before you could speak a word. Your toothless babble followed my unwavering voice. The sound of my love was unconditional collateral in the heart of my sacrifice.

Though I never proclaimed to be a skilled gardener like my grandmother, I knew how to sow mustard seeds so you would find the conviction to spring up into the strong man and the strong woman you are today. Sometimes a black mother has to just let the bud of their child push through on its own. My tears that watered you so you could grow toward the sun—a miraculous light source. I persisted in pulling up the common weeds that threatened to stunt your growth. My hands guided your maturity no matter what the road taken. A mother has to accept every morning as new mercy so that she may master the fine art of tending to wake-up calls, variable schedules, and the scraped knees of life before calling each day a good night.

All roads taken have led us here. Grace shaped you from birth to youth through adulthood. I had no blueprint other than prayer and perseverance to shelter your journey. The miracle of mother wit. My mother and her mother modeled what it took to raise a child; how to rise early to prepare the work of providing, and how to place a child's feet on solid ground and to train them up in the way they should go. Each of you possessed unique requisites and wishes. A mother has to know how to cultivate their children individually, according to their receptivity. A parent can never compare ourselves to the way our own parents and grandparents were raised, or the way they walked in their own stories. Their shoes we can never fill, but their experiences give us a reference point. I wore my own shoes when I discovered the kind of mother I wanted to be. There was no trying it on first to get the feel of it. One simply wears the size shoe you've been given. The resilience of knowing that the shoes of your journey will be tailored just for you. My shoes allowed me to walk into my own story as a strong mother.

You have to know there were no Zoom meetings on mothering then or lessons on how to love a son or daughter who undoubtedly will struggle to be independent of you while they secretly need you to be there every step of the way. And when that burst of liberation happens, let it. One day they will come to you and say, Thank you, Mom, when you least expect it.

Yes, I signed up to be a mother. A black mother carries cultural value and the weight of society's expectation. I carry no Ph.D. or a Pulitzer prize in mothering. I was entrusted with two gifts—a girl and a boy. I did not know what I was getting myself into. This calling. This raising of children redirects your life and focuses your attention to the details. Every side-eye angst, slamming of doors, or backtalk beneath the breath. Lord knows I had to make room for patience and communication, inspiration and humor. The sacrificing and prioritizing is in the planting of the seeds, watching them grow, and waiting for the unconventional to formally introduce itself. Like the day my daughter came home on a college break with a radiant glow. A mother knows her child. Call it a sixth sense about these things. My daughter and I walked that journey together and she received all the love and support she needed at home, surrounded by her village.

No home is perfect, but it is where a child learns to not be afraid to speak confidently about what concerns them. Like that time my son was a third-grader at a Christian elementary school. He told me that his white teacher made the black boys read passages from a Tom Sawyer book that contained the word nigger. It was obvious his teacher had not planted seeds of understanding in a room full of impressionable kids, who giggled while my son, and another boy who looked like him, stumbled over a word they knew they should not say. It was not their names. The teacher never explained prior to the reading what the word meant to her class or to herself. Troubled, I, along with other affected black parents, did not approve of this teacher's unacceptable approach. We requested a meeting with the principal. My son was let down by a teacher who was expected to build him up. It took several meetings with the principal, who reluctantly met with the teacher. Consequently, her contract was not renewed.

Nevertheless, we enrolled our son in another elementary school in fourth-grade with a better understanding of who he was and who he was not. Come what may, there will be arbitrary instances that need addressing in school. Like when the fourth-grade teacher implied that my black son had Attention Deficit Disorder because he was consistently talking or shifting in his seat. I didn't give any excuses but maybe my son was bored and needed the teacher to discern his learning style. However, at the parent-teacher conference my son's teacher leaned in to whisper "They can prescribe Ritalin. It really helps with focus." That was the one and only time I folded, thinking this woman knew my child better than I. But I was his mother, and took back my power and provided a healthy dose of checks and balances. My black son was going to be seen and heard without the world's cure for everything black.

So I went old school and made flashcard games to assist my son. And it never hurt to have a tutor in your toolkit. After all, it does take a village to raise a child.

I am that black mother who spread her wings, went back to school and continued being a role model to lead a way forward for her children. I burned the midnight oil. After working a full-time job. After cooking dinner. After helping my children with their homework. After their bedtime. It was my turn to study my college courses.

By middle school my son's voice had deepened into a rich tenor, and he used his new bass to test his influence. The elders used that phrase; You're beginning to smell yourself. It means someone is overconfident, or feeling as though they do not have to listen to an authority. My son had power in his voice as he towered over me at six feet in the eighth grade. But life is not based upon a person's height but the gravity of their reach. Sometimes, the expectations of society, and having to steer systems of stereotypes skewed a person's sense of worth. Especially children of color.

What mother would I be during my son's sophomore year in high school if I had not obtained a schedule of all of his classes so I could sit silently in each, for an entire day? All of his friends knew me, as I boldly walked the crowded hallways, navigating from classroom to classroom. I was not there just to observe my son's performance but to discern how his teachers showed themselves in relationship to black boys. Yes, I was that mother who cared enough to be the very best mother for him. I showed up ready to learn, as his teachers were schooled in the process.

When the coach recruited you as a sophomore to play varsity basketball, I was there to make sure your grades supported your hoop dreams. What mother would I be if I allowed the coach to take advantage of her black son whose mind was on basketball and not always on his grades? At six-feet-one my son was a force to be reckoned with, so when his grades rose up the coach sent my son from the bench to the floorboards with his right hand dribbling the ball to the paint, and the other hand held the loose elastic up on his narrow waist. I remember tip-toeing from the bleachers to the coach, politely interrupting his flow to ask why my son needed to hold up his shorts like someone on a street corner. Of course he was at a loss of words. Of course I suggested he find some duct tape to wrap around my son's gym shorts, so he could confidently continue shooting his shot like the star that he was. I gained the coach's respect after that.

There is nothing I would have done differently. After all we've been through, what other child would claim me?

And my darling daughter, what mother would I be if I did not champion for you?

You were a born cheerleader. During your junior high years, you were proud that I could make cheerleading outfits for you and your two best friends who cheered the boys' basketball team to winning. Those also were the times you made a quick change to don your own full-court gear, to bounce a ball to the rhythm of cheering audiences. Yes, I was that mother who let you stretch into the perfect fit of yourself.

Yes, there were growing pains, but I endured each season that seasoned me. My daughter arrived on the teen scene anxious about her appearance. What she wore was displayed on her body like a banner. After all, isn't the whole world looking? Or so we think. My daughter wore a green, button-up Polo shirt for every occasion. It was trending at the time, along with a new beeper of responsibility so she could inform us of her whereabouts on outings with friends. I clearly remembered the all-points bulletin when she had not made it home from school. I was at work and had not gotten her 3:40 pm on-the-dot phone call. But what mother would allow her daughter the freedom to spread her wings so she could be a part of the crowd? Me. Even though her so-called junior high friend fell short of having the best of intentions. That same friend boosted clothing from a department store for the thrill just to have another friend take the fall.

I remember you were among just a handful of blacks attending a predominantly white all-girl Catholic high school. You were proud to be on the Honor roll. Your mathematics teacher recommended you for honors Calculus next semester. But you come home from school one day upset because another white Calculus teacher refused to let you enroll in her class. She did not embrace the brown skin of your capacity. In fact, she sought to hinder your promotion. I witnessed the discouragement on your face and how you felt less confident about yourself. I decided to write a lengthy letter to your principal. My tasteful words highlighted the who, what, when and why my daughter was not allowed to participate in an honors class recommended by her math teacher. Needless to say, a week or so later, I received a phone call from the principal, followed by a letter offering her personal apology; informing me that my daughter had been placed in the honor's Calculus class for the next semester. To witness her fourteen-year-old face light up was priceless. Daughter, you never knew about that thirty-eight-year-old letter until I mentioned it just a few years ago.

That's what mothers do. We don't divulge everything at that moment. Why should we spoil it?

A mother volunteers and holds space to chaperone her black daughter and a large group of Excel students on a Civil rights tour to the South to experience the symbolisms of historical injustices; how this expedition shaped and fortified young minds. Or the trip she took to Ghana to stay with a host family. A mother exposes her children to a range of experiences and the intersectionality of embracing and understanding one's cultural heritage; and how the past and present are connected.

My children, if I have ever offended you by caring too much or gone off on some tangent to prove my point (and I have on several occasions), I apologize. But raising children is not for the weak. I admit, I have been both powerless as a mother and a courageous and passionate one for you. I have to represent and be an example of unwavering strength for you; barring those vulnerable moments. Parenting requires proficiency in trial and error, even your dad would attest to that. He loved you and was there until his last breath could no longer teach you how to grip the wheel of life; how to hold your head up and be a defensive driver; or how to stand to swing a golf club or shoot a "hail Mary" from mid-court.

Mothering is a full-time vocation with plenty of overtime. It is filled with joy and love, tears and wonder, and facts and fear. Part of nurturing is having to hold my tongue; to let my son purchase his first car at seventeen. Your powder-blue Chevy was your pride and joy. I knew it wasn't worth its coat of paint. Yet, I still let you make your own mistakes so that you would come to appreciate the value of a good dollar. I know your dad purchased your sister's first car because she was the oldest child. But you were on the cusp of manhood and needed reliable transportation for school and work. Sometimes, parents are on a need-to-know basis with their sons—there are those things they think we do not need to know. But I believe I had eyes in the back of my head. A village. I remember when you were being followed by a cop who also knew me. He did not pull you over when you made a wide right turn from the middle lane. He knew who you were—a black boy in his late teens trying to make it home. The world is full of police officers who will never extend grace to anyone outside the color of the blues.

I have written memories pressed against the flyleaf of my heart. I will never forget the victories or bumps in the road. I have dog-eared them and look back to see how far we have come. Like that time you, your sister and I all graduated the same year—you from high school and your sister from college. Daughter, your son was four-years-old when you and I received our bachelor degrees on the same day. Three weeks after the birth of my grandson you went back to school, carried a full-time job, increased responsibilities and all the possibilities.

A mother's job is to encourage their child's gift of language. When you both were younger, I read all the bedtime stories and tucked you in tight. I remember praying that you would share these precious memories with your own children.

Though I am not the perfect mother, I am perfect for you at any stage of your life. As my children, you blindly trusted my love and guidance and held on tightly.

Except the times you didn't.

I tried to hold you up, like a bicycle stand until you let go of your training wheels. And yes, you both wobbled but were determined to place one foot in front of the other to get from point A to point B. What mother would I have been if I had not let you fall? Neither of you wanted to get back up. I wanted to pick you up, wipe away your bruises and tears of a good struggle. What mother would I be if I had not supported your successes and encouraged your forward thinking? Your adolescent breakups, peer pressure, petty disagreements with your friends, and the opportunities you did not get are all part of the rhythm of life.

My mother used to tell me; Your attitude can hinder your altitude. Meaning that a negative or unmotivated mindset can prevent you from reaching your full potential.

There are times when you give excuses for why the bedroom isn't cleaned, why chores aren't done, or you-fill-in-the blank. But a mother's playbook is taken from many sources. When I worked at the medical school, a student gave me an impressive definition for the word excuse which was, excuses are tools of the incompetent used to build bridges to nowhere and monuments of nothingness, and those who specialize in them will seldom excel in anything else. You were encouraged to recite its meaning so you would understand how not to make them. It actually worked.

Every choice a mother makes is a prayer, a postponement or a persistent word spoken over their children's lives. Sometimes a mother has to handle the curve balls that come and make the perfect pitch to steer her child the right way. There are no perfect paths to take, because there will always be unexpected detours or dead-end road decisions to make.

There are things a child never speaks of to their parents. And that's okay. You're an adult now but my wish for you is to take those embarrassing feelings you did not share with me, and disclose to your own children; my grandchildren, to help them resolve their own puzzles.

I am that black mother who gave you the talk before you entered this cruel world and throughout your lives. A mother cannot be too careful. So I write this letter to say I'm proud of who you have become. I love you and would never change anything about your upbringing because I am still lifting you up.

The icing on the cake is that I get to experience you making it known that what I have done for you is appreciated. It is a reminder that there may be strikes in a child's life, but certainly a mother can never count their child out.

With a loving embrace,

Mom

Sandra Rivers-Gill

On Toilet Angels: An Essay on Parenting

Dear Kid,

Its skirt is no bigger than my closed fist; it is made of peach and white yarn woven through a plastic cone grid. I am not sure where it came from but I imagine a church craft fair a few decades ago. Its wings and head are floppy, knitted (or perhaps crocheted, I am not an artisan who can tell the difference), held with no reinforcements that would behold a more proper angel. This angel looks nowhere quite directly, neither down from the heavens with curiosity or compassion nor up from the earth with pleading, desperate eyes. She is not prayerful.

—

You should know that when we moved in with my father, I was as stunned as anyone. My wife, your second mom, was taking the move in stride, relieved to be back on the East Coast but in a town more financially forgiving than her home of Queens. You were excited to live with Papa and even more so once you discovered the decades-old tradition of watching *Wheel of Fortune* before bed with a grandparent. But I sat in my teenage bedroom, walls no longer adorned with Doors and Nirvana posters, and felt the gastric rush beneath my sternum as I wondered, "What did I do?"

I had a job—tenured, unionized, paying a solid middle-class salary—and a little house we could afford on just my income. I had amazing friends, a yoga practice, trails where I could bike for miles that stretched flat before me, not a single gear needing to be changed. But six months before, my wife was clear: I had every symptom of burnout. I was forgetful, disinterested, impatient. My depression was not swayed by medication, therapy, meditation, or movement. Burnout was a new messy roommate, and I couldn't get out of bed.

This job had become toxic. My students no longer showed up to class; when they did, they never came prepared. My colleagues whispered in hushed tones about the next round of budget cuts or what department was next on the conservative state's chopping block. My research funds were near non-existent and my next chance to apply for sabbatical was seven years away. I had to leave this job.

But here, in this 1,300 square foot New England cape with its slanted bedroom walls (perfect for gazing at an upside-down Kurt Cobain and Jim Morrison in my sullen teenage years) and single bathroom was not where I thought I would end up. After college, after the years in and out of the eating disorder clinic, after coming out to my parents (who assured me they would "pray for me"), after drinking my way through two graduate degrees and five years pre-tenure, I would never have thought this bedroom would be one that I would share with my wife. I would never have thought you would take the room across the hall where my sister once kept her porcelain dolls, prom dress and AP Calculus text. Her purple walls now watch over dinosaurs and Pokémon cards.

The bathroom, once submitted to a five-person shower rotation and filled with more shampoo, conditioner and bodywash bottles than our current plastics crisis can handle, was now the domain of you, an eight year old boy, and a seventy-two year old man.

My wife and I used the renovated shower stall in the basement.

My father was still preaching, my wife was still resistant to formal religion, you were still in need of ADHD medication and I was still sullen. But also, in the first month "home," I began to feel my breath get a little deeper.

—

We've been buying toilet paper by the pallet from Costco for years—before the infamous pandemic toilet paper shortage. Between that and their controversial rotisserie roast chicken, we were nervous about moving away from our Midwest home and losing access to these staples. So perhaps it was serendipitous to learn that Maine's only Costco opened up just a town over from us a few months before our move.

The day after we unloaded our cars into my dad's house, filling his basement with dog and cat necessities, our modest wardrobes that could cover three seasons of Maine's weather, and the half dozen books we culled from our library of hundreds now making its way across the country in a storage pod, we drove to Costco. We filled up on the usual.

And replenished my dad's toilet paper supply.

The first month of adjusting to one another, particularly around mealtimes, led me to feel some of the old adolescent rumblings. Dad would fill his side of the fridge with beer. He would insist that he cook his dinner first so he could watch the news. He would be late cooking his dinner, which would push back our dinner and your bedtime. He would be angry if I bought too much fruit from the store—there simply wasn't the counter space. One afternoon, his face contorted furiously as I stood unloading groceries from the car, he erupted first. "I just cannot use your sandpaper toilet paper. I don't know where you get it, but it is not good for my hemorrhoids!" I nodded sullenly and did my best to keep my mouth shut and not instigate more fury. "I am going to keep my own toilet paper on the back of the toilet. For myself." He walked heavily back into the house, leaving me to carry in my own groceries.

The next time I visited the bathroom, the peach and cream angel was on top of the toilet tank, her skirt balanced on top of a plush, quilted roll.

Over the next few days, as the roll decreased in girth, her skirt concealed the paper, shielding it from your eight-year-old's unwieldy overspray.

—

Cat finished her PhD in the middle of the pandemic, the spring of 2020. She did not don a gown and attend a ceremony. We held a fire pit gathering in our backyard; a BYOB and BYO-chair event offering s'more fixings in sealed plastic bags. But we were ecstatic. What we didn't tell our friends who gathered in our driveway that evening was that finishing her dissertation was the final hurdle we were waiting for before beginning our foster care certification classes. We were eager to become parents and with graduate school out of the way, we could finally make the time to be in one state long enough to complete our classes, CPR certifications, and background checks. We were stable.

Many universities will offer partner hires to spouses of tenured faculty who have the qualifications for a teaching and research position. Two of my cis-gendered, straight colleagues were offered partner hires the years that Cat and I were denied. There was no explanation. At the second rejection, there was even an open position for someone with her expertise. She was already teaching for that department. Her research and teaching dossier were overlooked. She just wasn't in the budget. And, as my Dean shouted across the lawn at me as she rushed to another meeting, "You guys are actually married, right? That will help." That didn't help.

These rejections meant that Cat would have to pivot away from her expertise; if we were going to stay local to become parents, she would have to give up her professional career. Pivot to a new industry. She sent dozens of applications before a friend interviewed and offered a part-time position in communications for a nonprofit.

This is enough for us to get by as parents. We could pay the mortgage and the grocery bill. And still afford takeout once every few weeks.

—

Dad is harried again. He storms from the bathroom, breathing heavily, holding the toilet angel high in his left hand. You and I are practicing reading at the table.

"Why, may I ask," Dad pauses to take a deep breath, audibly modulating his voice, "is this angel on the bathroom floor?"

I shrug my shoulders and return my gaze to my finger and the word I am trying to get you to sound out. Your eyes are wide, his lips are quivering. You are looking straight at the angel.

"Cameron?" my Dad says, shaking the angel.

"I don't know!" Your cheeks are wet with tears.

"Do not move this angel. Ever." Dad turns on his heel and walks back down the hall.

I pat you on the back; it is unclear to me why my dad is so angry about the toilet paper angel. "It's okay, bud, "I whisper. "You didn't know."

You stutter and try to catch your breath, turning your nose into my shoulder. "I can't go to the bathroom with it looking at me."

—

The phone calls were constant.

You were constantly being called oppositional.

We were denied an IEP meeting.

You were suspended. Three times. In first grade.

The state had made this illegal, suspending kids under third grade.

I sent an open letter to everyone who would read it, including the superintendent, citing these laws.

The school vice principal told me, when I marched into her office after the second suspension, that I could cite my research and she would go out and find her own research to support her view.

I told her research didn't work that way. I asked her if she knew what peer-reviewed research was. (This is the part of the story where Cat tells me I go off the rails as a PhD. Though she giggles as she says this).

The Vice Principal said, "I am sure you are going to tell me."

To which my only response was, "Well, are you going to listen?"

Nothing gets accomplished in this meeting. I said things like "school-to-prison pipeline" and she said things like "Now he is hearing this from his parent—which one are you? I can't keep you two straight—so of course he thinks he is being treated unfairly."

I audio-recorded this meeting. The state had a single-consent law for recording. It's legal. And these are actual words she said.

You and I walked out holding hands. I explained to you that what you did in school was against the rules and you needed a consequence; but I also explained that I was sad you would miss school because you deserved to be in school like every other kid. All kids deserved school.

All you said was, "I know I am a bad boy. I am not a school kid."

—

"Why is this on the floor again?" my dad asks.

The silence that follows between you and I, both of us are nailed to our seats staring at the peach and cream blur jutting from my dad's waving hand.

We say nothing.

"I am just going to have to put this away now. It won't be in the bathroom if you keep putting it on the floor."

As Dad turns to bring the toilet angel to his room—I guess she will be a dresser angel now— I look at you. Your torso loosens. I smile. We let it go.

—

I do not expect to cry at your IEP meetings. The first one, where you were denied any formal interventions (and we were told "We will do everything that would be in one of those anyway"), it had only been a few weeks since my mom had passed. All I could think about was how I wanted to talk to her, to find out how she would phrase her questions to the school team. How she might push back against their denial of services. How she might be sweet and tough in the perfect ratio.

She went into special education with a firm belief that all kids deserved access to education, regardless of what it takes to get there. Born in the 1950's, she was raised alongside her mother's youngest sister, Joyce. Joyce had intellectual assessments that denied her much of what would become legally mandated in the years after my mother graduated from college. Joyce and my mom did everything together when they were young, including Girl Scouts and Saturday matinees. They all lived with my great grandparents, sharing a pull-out sofa bed and weathering Vermont's winters in homemade miniskirts and wool hand-me-down jackets. I know my mom was shaped by Joyce's life—her humor, her friendship, and the schooling she was denied.

As the youngest, I was the last of my sisters living at home. Having recently hit menopause, my mom turned from a life-long tea drinker to Dunkin Donuts regular with cream and sugar, blowing through the backdoor after school with Styrofoam cup in hand, shoulderbag full of files and evening homework in the other. If I were on the living room floor working on my own homework, she would settle into her rocking chair and begin sharing her last ten hours of meetings—students from another school district becoming vivid, lovable characters in my imagination, parents becoming sympathetic foils, administrators the nemesis of progress and resources. At her funeral, we learned that she was consistently thought to be "too kind" and I wonder if kind means effective?

Our recent IEP meeting began with a declaration. "We love your kid," says the school's special education director. "He belongs here. And we are going to wrap around him."

When you walk in ten minutes later to tell us you are going to your classroom, you stop to hug almost every adult around the table.

—

After eight months, we move out. We buy a small ranch with a big price tag, question if it is the smartest decision in the Trump landscape and spend two months painting and rehabbing floors. I have a job in research. For now, anyway. When we move, we bring a pallet of Costco toilet paper and set a wooden frog on the back of the toilet seat.

When we visit my dad for pizza and *Wheel of Fortune* night, the toilet angel is back on her perch, looking nowhere and everywhere at once.

Ally Day

In the period of time before becoming a parent, I reflected on moments in my own childhood where the recall was joyful and pure. Investigation, Jumping, Ritual are three works from a larger lithographic print series considering life in the domestic space. From the child's point of view, the everyday concerns were informed by others around them shaping memories that will stand in for segments of time.

Maggie Denk-Leigh

Investigation, lithograph, 2004

Jumping, lithograph, 2003

Ritual, lithograph, 2004

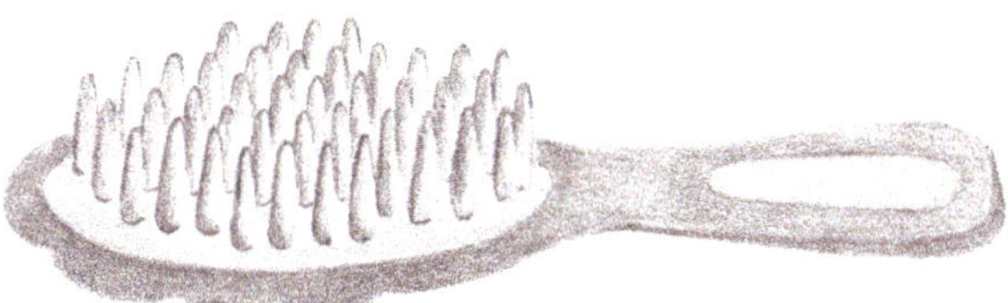

Letter to My Children

Dear September, November, and January,

I have kept track of our lives for years in notebooks. On every page I tell myself to be a good dad. To make good food for you to eat, to take long walks with you, to check your homework and pack your lunches, to learn to love the things you love, to give you room to grow, to answer your questions, to think before I act, to believe every word you say.

"8/6/2009 Yesterday was baby day. Went to Toledo Hospital for our first ultrasound: there's the beautiful profile—nose, lips, chin, little cheeks—and there's the dinosaur spine curled like a comma in the womb; I could see all four chambers of the heart, and I could watch it pulse and squeeze and send all the good blood flowing to brain and fingertips."

There was a time when I didn't want to be alive anymore. I wished I could fall asleep but not wake up, that maybe I could be taken in the night by an angel of the Lord and never rise from sleep to face a new day. In this life there will be small moments that exist as embers in your memory, and something in your day will trigger a nourishing gust that make those memories flare up and brighten and warm your spirit. You will find your way into the next chore and through the end of it with that light and heat to guide you. For me, back in that time of dread, and even today when the dread comes on me again, there were three embers couched against raging winds and driving rains, and those embers were fuel, and those embers were you, my three babies, September, November, and January.

In the dark night at the end of a long gravel driveway I sit in my car. I've turned the key off, but the radio continues to play for a few minutes before the power cuts out. I don't remember what I'm listening to, but I do remember wondering how fast I'd have to drive my car into a wall to end it all. The mail is on the seat next to me. It's mostly things I don't want to look at—bills I can't pay, letters for a former resident, post cards advertising new windows and one for a behavioral health treatment center. I look up and I can see into our house. The yellow kitchen glow is warm. My plants are on the wide shelf under the window. The dining room table is covered with evidence of a bustling life. November and January, earlier you played with the brothers who live up the hill and your sister had track practice. She's in her room doing homework, and November, you're in bed trying to fall asleep even though January is talking like a tree full of magpies.

Small things will save you—believe me—recognizing the Carolina chickadee's song, remembering the teacher who taught you how to spell 'definitely,' singing every word to a favorite song—sometimes these are the gusts of wind that make the embers flare. The small things that saved me on that day? The post card with the behavioral health center's phone number on it that I called the next morning, a scrap of paper tucked in my notebook with September's handwriting on it, "Table was cleared when I left", an orange crayon drawing November made of a dragon "60 feet long!" and a letter I wrote to January, three years old, describing him as he is now so he knows what he used to be like when he reads this years later.

"5/17/2016 On another note, January never stops crying. Maybe I'll give him a little more bottle and turn that fan on."

"12/30/2016 This morning the horned larks are flying in their flocks around and over the farmyard and gathering at the end of the driveway and I've made stock from the ham and chicken left over from Christmas dinner."

When I talked to the therapist I said, "I'm afraid I'm going to drown. I'm afraid I'm going to grow to hate my kids, my wife, my whole life. I feel like I'm suffocating and even their brightness doesn't feel like it'll lead me out of this dark place. When I talked to the therapist, I told her, "I want to feel better. I want to feel normal. I never want to leave my babies."

I write everything down. I have done so for years. I collect your questions and jokes, your good and bad days, your drawings on scraps of paper, your wonder and astonishment, and all your grievances in my little notebooks. These are my kindling—fuel for the days the dread comes over me. If I could give you only one piece of advice, I would say: Write your life down. In the margins of your notebook paper, on the blank end pages of your novel, in a dedicated notebook, or on post-it notes you hang under your monitor, write your life down. You will find jokes your friends told you, funny things your children said, recipes you loved eating at holiday get togethers, the calculus of difficult relationships recorded in your journal will give you the solution to loving your partner better in the here and now.

"5/17/2019 The boys insist on my presence and thank God for them if only for that reason. They make me act and therefore live much better than I think I could do on my own in this situation."

My children, I saw a something on Instagram that I never stop thinking about; it's this post: People say all the time, "I'd die for my children." Okay, but would you live for them? Actually live. Make better choices. Try practicing sobriety. Take better care of yourself physically and mentally? Your kids don't need you to die for them. They need you to live. I read entries in my journal describing our adventures together. Creek stomping. Fishing. Going to September's volleyball games and track meets. Hot chocolate and Tiger Beat at Borders books when September was just a 9-year-old girl and November was sleeping in his carrier. Brother's Day, a holiday that January made up for him and November to celebrate. Reading comics. Playing Lego Star Wars. November's three weeks in the hospital. January born on a record setting cold day. When I am cold and barren, I can turn to these memories stacked like cord wood in my bookshelf and feed the low fire burning in my spirit. I have lived. I stayed here. All this time I have lived and it's because of you.

"10/5/2009 I need a break. A day outside or something. A day without thinking. You need a day to be weightless. I love you. There's that hard warm fact that holds me together."

"But I always think that the best way to know God is to love many things."
Vincent Van Gogh

If you ever feel the dread I refer to, and you'll know, please understand that there is nothing wrong with you. You were made according to a whim or a plan we can't understand but you were not made broken. You are whole, and the dread is only a part of you but not all of you. Some people call it the black dog. My family has a whole pack of black dogs, one for each of us. Is there one for each of you? September's dog is black as obsidian and sharp as winter winds. November's dog is black as coal and plumes like Victorian England. January's dog is black as night and has a scar over its right eye. I don't know. It's not as if you can hear them sniffing at the door or knocking garbage cans over in the night. They just show up and lick your brain, chew memories like so much jerky, piss on your celebrations, and chase off the sun like the wolf Sköll in Norse Mythology.

You will want to know who will save you from the black dogs, what will save you? I say writing. Memory. Put everything down in the notebook that makes you feel some goodness in your heart. Capture every day! In 2009 I wrote, "Make a poem for the walk I took last May in the woods on Silica Road—'Hazardous Conditions May Exist.' I start the poem:

I ignored 'hazardous conditions may exist'
in the floodplain of Ten-Mile Creek,
the unblossomed hazards of the old dump
that threaten to bloom as blood and bruises
if I take a bad step. I know there are coiled springs
and rusty kitchen knives buried under ground.
This is where my dad brought our garbage
in the bed of his pick-up truck and flung it out

That's all I wrote but I remember that day thanks to those few lines. I saw a scarlet tanager in the canopy—the first and only one I've ever seen. The lines took me back even further, to when I was a boy younger than January, helping my dad unload the truck at the dump. He hates snakes. He reached down for a bag of trash but grabbed a garter snake three feet long, it must have been hiding in a roll of wet carpet. With a shout he flung the snake across the dump. It writhed in the air as it flew, creating strange calligraphy that I later identified as the first letters of poetry I ever read.

"2/09/2010 I look at my son, my son John never met, and say John, he is new to this world, and the whole world under the sun, under you wherever you have gone when all things end, is new to him. He is discovery, fat and flush. Every outburst a Eureka! moment. He faces the peril of the unknown undaunted."

"8/2009 Tonight we cut open a musk melon and September ate the whole thing."

Years later you will look at these words and you'll be so glad you kept them.

Maybe your grandparents will die before you have children, as mine did. Maybe the only way your children will ever know the rest of their family is by reading your memories. As I say, the notebooks are kindling for warm fires blazing in your spirit. You will need their light. You will need these memories—they will do two things, at least. They will take you back to happy times and you will be reminded how good it is to be alive. For me, I can smell that fresh cut musk melon and hear the singular sound of a sharp knife sliding through and hitting the cutting board at the end of its journey. On your grimmest days it will remind you how far you've traveled. You'll want to know that—how much you've already endured and how so much of it's behind you, how the difficulties didn't last but you did.

There's a third dreadful reason to keep these words. You'll have a record of who you've outlived. Some of us let the black dog eat. You don't know your maternal great grandma, but she let the black dog grind her down like a strip of rawhide. Your grandma Luci whose love for everyone seemed unquenchable let her fire die, drowned under the black dog's heavy streams of piss. She just quit life one day. None of us know why. I can say that I won't be like them that I can leash the dog and live. I have evidence. I have outlived both sets of my mother's teeth.

I have lived in fear for so long. I say to my therapist, "What if my children hate me when they're adults? What if they collect broken promises like worthless coins in a purse?"

I didn't know what neglect really was until I was thirty-eight years old. Did you know that someone can say, "I love you," but still neglect you? As if saying it is sufficient for all our needs. As if saying it replaces affection. As if saying it fills the hungry belly. As if saying it tucks you in at night. As if saying it comforts the aching heart. As if saying it is the only evidence you need. As if saying it is an apology for unresolved conflict. As if saying it fills the hours. As if saying it teaches you a skill you'll need later in life.

Love is action. Neglect is inaction. Action is the antidoted for despair. When you work, do a good job. When you're in love, hold nothing back. Sing your favorite songs out loud and often. Go to the doctor, take your medicine and keep track of your progress. Wear clean underwear. Eat breakfast. Brush your teeth. Drink plenty of water. This is action. This is not neglect. The black dog may come but it won't be able to stay long. You'll be too busy passing your light around.

"Things that matter most must never be at the mercy of things that matter least."
Goethe

I love you in all ways,

Dad

Michael Kocinski

Elliott

Dear Elliot,

When I painted *Trans Womb* in 2023, it was purely an intellectual project. It completed my set of reproductive justice themed art. It made the point that lots of things in nature are not binary, nor do things in nature remain the same. I was proud of the painting for how it made this subtle trans-affirming point through art, but I did not have an emotional connection to the painting.

But now—thanks to you and your gender transition—when I see this painting, I have a completely different response. I no longer think of it just as a statement on the facts of gender and sex diversity, of natural variety, of what is known. It also symbolizes the immense potential of the unknown, all that is still becoming and was, "everything everywhere all at once." Before you, I simply did not know that being trans was really all about becoming joy.

I wish I would have seen it sooner, and it will always be ironic to me that I didn't. I'm a lifelong feminist. I have many trans friends. I'm a Women's Studies professor for goodness sakes! But when you told me in 2023 that you thought you may be a boy, I admit that I had doubt. I wasn't upset, and I was able to be immediately supportive. I could jump right into "support trans child" mode, finding you a supportive LGBTQ+ affirming therapist, encouraging you to do research, talking to the teachers for you about your new name and pronouns, etc. But, at the beginning at least, I was doing these supportive things as a rational, moral response because I respect your rights to your body. I wasn't sure where this was going or what would happen.

You were always more of a "tomboy" than your siblings, but I'm pretty sure you would have cut anyone who took away your shiny red heels or snappy purse. When I think of little you, I see you in your disheveled pink Princess Aura dress, muddy, red Lightning McQueen rain boots, breathless but happy from rounding up chickens and climbing the mulberry tree. So, while I certainly saw "masculinity" and "boyness" in you from the start, I didn't know if transitioning to Elliot meant leaving the red heels behind.

But you left something else behind.

When you were little, you had sometimes debilitating sensory processing problems. Finding the "right" clothing was a nightmare. Shirts and underwear were particularly daunting. The cut, feel, fabric, color, flow all had to be just right for it to work, and even then, sometimes it was all too much for you and you had a meltdown. We tried hard to accommodate. We gave up on underwear often, and we were able to find a handful of clothes that worked for you, but the hunt for more clothes was perpetual and tense. I once even tried forcing you after the grandparents on both sides made comments about how Jess and I really needed to get you to wear underwear. But holding you down and forcing clothes on your little screaming body was too gut-wrenching. Commando reigned the day.

As you matured from toddler to child, you were able to take more control over your clothes and the textures on your body and things got a bit better. You wore both "boy" and "girl" clothes because the "feel" of the shirt or underwear was what was important, and being feminist parents, we were fine with that. But you were still always prone to outbursts and meltdowns. Even a good shirt could go wrong if it rained. You could not stand being wet in clothes so avoided getting rained on like nobody's business. You were the only five-year-old at the ready with a *Paw Patrol* umbrella.

But when you couldn't be ready, when you were overstimulated, or when Jess or I didn't see it coming, a sensory thing could completely derail you. You would burst into tears, thrash, scream wildly, sometimes hitting or throwing. You were unable to regulate your response.

Being "good," disability-positive parents, Jess and I tried getting you help for the symptoms without getting a diagnosis. This was the great autism awakening in the United States. Everyone, I mean everyone, was talking about the autism spectrum. Sensory processing disorder is part of this spectrum, but we did not want to expose you to Applied Behavior Analysis (ABA) or other therapies that focused on making your behaviors more acceptable to others. We did, however, want to make sensory processing less traumatic to you. So, we focused on occupational therapy and talk therapy to give you all sorts of tools to manage how your body felt with fabric. By the time you were eight or so, clothes and shoes were still a trigger but no longer a guarantee for a meltdown. The near daily breakdown over something touching your body gradually reduced to a trickle, popping up only a couple times a month. I figured we had settled into an adapted routine based on our better awareness of your physical needs. You have sensory processing disorder, but we could mitigate and avoid triggering fabrics and outfits, and you had tools for stress management if you were triggered.

But as I watched you transition to Elliot over these last two years, your meltdowns have nearly disappeared. More than that, joy has emerged inside you.

At first, when you started to try more clothes and styles as part of the transition, I was worried because of how hard it always has been to find any clothes. After over a decade of a very, very particular style of track pants/leggings as the only acceptable pants, I couldn't imagine you being able to wear blue jeans, let alone a chest binder. But your wardrobe exploded.

Today you wear khakis and jeans, track pants, and cargo shorts. You can select a shirt off the rack—off the internet for goodness sakes!—and just wear it. There are no tears about not being able to wear the shirt you love because it doesn't feel right. You are no longer stressed about the little hairs on your neck when I cut your hair.

I know your skin still takes in textures, pressure, and temperatures just a little bit differently. Lots of noise, people, and lights can add to the sensory overload. And, when you are extremely exhausted and overstimulated, sensory issues suddenly become a very big deal. But it is, without a doubt, markedly different now. Last week, I watched you rollerblade in the rain.

As you've transitioned, you left behind discomfort.

Now you look like a teenage boy, and you look more like a man every day. Your teachers call you Elliot. Your friends know you are trans and love you. In fact, I've watched you become one of those "cornerstone" friends. The guy everyone in the school respects and knows. The guy friends go to for help and advice and support. I've seen you support dozens of your peers through their own meltdowns, and with grace and impressive maturity, accept and move through your own meltdowns if they happen.

With discomfort removed, you've literally blossomed. You are confident and bold, but also so understanding and open to others, to the world, and yourself. A beautiful masculine strength has grown from you, one that guides, holds space for others, and is open to the unknown. Rather than a patriarchal, hegemonic mode, the masculinity that has emerged from you is responsive, ever changing, full of potential and life.

Now when I look at the *Trans Womb* painting, I realize I had it all wrong. The point isn't just that sex and gender are naturally variable. The point is the potential, the brightness, the unknown that the changers, like you, make visible. The natural world is full of beautiful transitions, and they are nothing to fear. The becoming, the process of being, is the joy that trans people and all gender "troublemakers" offer the world. They offer the promise of infinite potential. Trans people literally manifest joy.

So, I still don't know if you will ever wear red shiny heels again, but now I see how limited the question itself was. It isn't about the past or even the future, but the joy in being able to do what you want with your body. I want to see and nourish each choice you make with your body. Thank you for letting me step into the unknown with you so I could see the full beauty of trans joy.

Love,

Mommy Sarah

Trans Womb Description:
Trans Womb features flowers that change sex, like the Dungowan Bush Tomato (the first plant recognized as "gender fluid") and Jack-In-The-Pulpit, and plants that are both male and female, such as the Tulip and Petunia.
See *Trans Womb* at https://www.feministslut.com/

As a Mother Guards Her Child, Her Only Child

Dear Naima,

I have had to pee since July of 2015.

Your bones are made of grapes and crab meat.

Your blood is made of lemon juice and garlic.

There was a day when a knowing came over me that I would be the mom to one dark-haired girl.

She would be a culture keeper.

She would sing and dance.

I knew you would be the picture of compassion, a citizen of the world.

Two of your first words were "Bob Dylan"

Dear Naima,

When you were a year and a half old, I left you for the first time. We spent two nights and 3 days away from each other, and I thought I might die. I wanted to leave the meditation retreat I paid for and committed to. I even moved my car from the parking lot where I would be blocked in so that if I couldn't control myself, and simply had to come to you, I wouldn't need to ask anyone to move their car. I called your Dad and told him I wanted to go home. For some reason, there was no electricity in our apartment that weekend, so you and he stayed at Grandma and Grandad's house. He convinced me to stay and to be strong. It was the Spring after the election of 2016. I was in mourning over that and the death of a dear friend. You and I were still nursing, and I was so afraid that the days away would wean you. I wasn't ready.

I had a private room and brought a few personal items to make it feel like home. I had my Toledo quilt and my robe, some of your Dad's artwork, probably some Nag Champa. Throughout the weekend, I went up to my room to be among my things and get a taste of home. I was missing you so much, and my breasts filled up with milk. I cried and cried and cried. I grieved. I was tapping into a cosmic homesickness I have felt since my earliest memories.

On the last day, I was on the homestretch. I knew I would see you soon. I went to my room for one of my fabricated errands, to get tea or to fill my water bottle. As I put the key in the door, it occurred to me that my home was not in that room, even if my robe and blanket were. Home was in my heart. It resides within.

At the very end of the retreat, when we broke silence and people shared insights, I told of that sense. The teacher looked proud and said, "That's foundational."

I want you to have that foundation. I want you to know that your home is in your heart. I don't want you to feel that homesickness, cosmic or otherwise. I know you have a right to an injury or trauma to heal because that is part of being human. But I hope it's not that one. I hope you always know that you are connected to the center of the Earth. And I hope that connection offers you peace and well-being beyond anything human relationships can. When I got home from the retreat, I met you and your Dad on the street in front of the house. I walked up behind you and got down on the ground to give you a flower I brought with me. You turned around and looked at me like, "Where have you been?".

Dear Naima,

When you were in 3rd grade you started riding the school bus home for the first time. Every day, I wanted to run out the front door to greet you. I wanted to run down the sidewalk. I walked out of the house barefoot because I couldn't wait to get to you. I went outside in the bitter cold in a T-shirt because I couldn't wait to see you. I couldn't wait to feel your cheeks and your forehead. I wanted to hug you and take you into my arms and make you warm and safe all day, every day.
I know what it means now to be sure I will be with you forever. In this world, or from another plane. I will never leave you. When you are two streets over at a friend's house, or I am an airplane flight away from you, I miss you the same.
I have missed you since you left my body.

What will I do with the years between when you leave home and when I move back into yours? Will our fates take us back to the house where we were both born?

Will I help you with your children there? I promise to be a present grandparent. To soak in the cravings for babies with yours. I will be playful, loving, and helpful.

They tell us to take ourselves away from you. To push you from the nest. To teach you independence. I am telling you now that if you need me to lie in your bed to help you fall asleep until the night before you leave for college, warm up my pillow because I'll be there. Also, if you want to live at home while you're in college, please do. Also, don't go to college if you don't want to.

Dear Naima,

How could I avoid giving you my fears and misunderstandings of how to live?

How would I unknow what I knew enough to teach you differently?

I don't think I have.

I don't know what you think of me. I wonder about it all the time.

Do I seem confident about anything at all? Do I seem sure of myself? Because that's what I want for you, but how do I model what I don't have?

How do I teach you that your body is perfect when I was taught that being overweight was the worst thing ever?

I have been so clumsy when it comes to talking with you about body image. Periods? Pooping? Fevers? I'm cool. But, the F word? The one that made my mom hate herself? The one I was always afraid to be, and then when I was, it really wasn't that bad? I don't know how to talk to you about it.

You were very young when you hinted at worrying about it yourself. And other people around us were not as sensitive as me. I always say everyone's body is perfect. We don't make comments about other people's bodies. There are more interesting things to mention about a person besides whether or not they have gained or lost weight. The preoccupation is disturbing. We are more than our BMI.

You will be beautiful for your whole life. I want you just to know that. I never did. And never really was. Certainly, no one ever told me that I was. So, I had to be other stuff. Funny, smart, talented, needy, insecure. Always over-compensating.

Everyone thinks you are beautiful, AND you already are other stuff. People will love you and hate you, and it will be for unhealthy and healthy reasons.

Dear Naima,

You longed for siblings, to be a big sister. I didn't want you to share me with other kids. I only have enough love for you.

Every time you asked me to have a baby, we got a kitten.

Dear Naima,

When your Dad and I got married, your Grandad said, "Let there be peace on Earth, and let it begin with me."

He was talking about the multicultural life we were starting.

And about the intercultural baby in my belly.

I don't want you to be a Muslim or a Jew.

I want you to be Naima.

I don't want you to rely on other people's laws and beliefs defined ages ago to develop your relationship with god.

Religion makes a person hate themselves and the things they love.

Tradition, judgment, and labeling things "sin" are not ways to have a relationship with God.

Organized religion and marriage are tools of oppression used by the patriarchy to subjugate women and divide and control people.

If I believed in Satan, I would say convincing people that their path to God was through.

Religion was his most masterful trick.

Never forget that God is not a man.

Women grow life in our bodies.

We are creators.

Never let them make you afraid of your power.

Never let them make you feel small.

Rely on your inner knowing.

Welcome your spirit to empower and elevate you to the highest expression of your Self.

Be guided by your inner voice.

Tune in and never lose the channel.

You told me once that God is your dance teacher. That is all you ever need to know.

Dear Naima,

What did we put in your head about money when sometimes we could buy what we needed, but other times we were "waiting on a paycheck"? Sometimes we were waiting for months or even seasons.

What did you learn about working too hard for not enough money?

What did you learn about being a creative person trying to make a living and do work you care about? Were you aware of how hurt I was when my city took my work for granted? Or did you see the joy I also felt at being able to honor Toledo's art and culture? I know you had fun at Jazz festivals.

Remember the day I bought us all new pillows? I had just gotten the best job of my life, and it had nothing to do with art.

Will you be an accountant like your Dad wants?

Or will you be a school counselor/nail tech/fashion designer/dancer/who works in a nursing home?

I think the latter group.

Be well-rounded. Be creative and also have another way to make money. As much as it pains me to admit that there is no other way to do it, there is no other way to do it. OR… be a star.

Dear Naima,

Do you and will you understand my introversion? Did you have trouble understanding why I dreaded parties and how it was such a feat for me to be at events? Why I go to my room when we have company, after making sure everyone has what they need?

I have never felt like I belonged anywhere. Being alone has always meant safety for me. If there is no one nearby to hurt me or for me to hurt, that is what I seek out.

Did you understand when I couldn't get out of bed? You treated me so gently on those days.

You had a quiet understanding beyond your maturity.

Did you know I was always trying my best, and will that be enough for you? Because knowing that about my parents has not been enough for me.

I insist I am trying harder.

Will that be enough to avoid my most dreaded fate, that you will feel about me the way I feel about my mother?

But, I promise I'll never be jealous of your happiness.

I fucking promise.

Rebecca was in a play that I wanted to take you to, but it was too grown-up at the time. In it, her character talked about her grandmother, who died at age 36 of melancholia. I know why that happened. I do not want you to understand with the same depth why that happens to women. Why we die of melancholia. I do not want you to live a life where you feel mistreated, taken for granted, used, taken advantage of, and spiritually and financially beaten down to the point of destruction, and then made to feel crazy for saying you won't stand for it anymore. I don't want you to ever question your known reality. I don't want you to think it is your job to endure so that the men around you can succeed due to your support and sacrifice.

It was dicey there for a minute when your Dad and I were breaking up.
How much damage did that time do to you? You had to take care of me, and I hated it, but I couldn't function. I needed you to be strong, and I couldn't be strong for you, and I hated myself for it. When did you get to feel your feelings? How will that play out for you later? Will you sniff it out and see it coming? Will you walk into it or away from it? Will you hate me for being so mad at your Dad that I couldn't keep it separate? Will you fall in love with women as I so strongly suggest? Will you escape the patriarchy at least a little bit?

My grandma used to say she felt sorry for my husband.

I didn't care about learning to cook or dust.

Now, I cook, still don't dust, and my husband was the luckiest man alive with not a single need unmet for ten years until I had the strength to leave.

I have joked the same thing about you. You might be accustomed to getting whatever and anything you want. The poor guy. But, I take it back. I do not feel sorry for him. He should be so fortunate as to get to be near you and experience you. You are a marvel. You should have everything and whatever you want. So should I.

I want you to attract and be attracted to people who respect you and treat you with kindness.

Tell the others to fuck off.

Dear Naima,
If you ever detect impatience in my voice or my response to you, please understand that I am simply exhausted and it's not you who makes me tired. It is the endless requirement to make all the decisions and have all the answers. To think of everything and be responsible for holding up the world. It is being full of power and yet having no power. It is taking care of everyone around me and wondering whose job it is to take care of me. By the way, it's not your job.

Dear Naima,

When you were in the NICU, the nurses told me they had never seen a mom pump so much colostrum. I gave them bottles and bottles and bottles. I considered it my only purpose in life to nourish you even as I wept while we were apart those tender first days after you were born. When we went to your six-month check-up, your Doctor commented on how much you had grown. I was glad to hear it, of course. And then she said, "That's all you, Rachel. With your milk." It was one of my proudest moments in life. When you were 22 months old, you took your last sip of nutrition from my body. You walked up to me and lay down in my lap. I gave you my boob, and you took one taste, said "Ew" and got up and walked away. That was it.

Dear Naima,

If I ever made you feel like there was anything in the world more important than you, I felt it every time and didn't know how to manage it.

I created lots of things before you were born.

Work is very important to me.

I wanted you to see me creating and working for my city and my community.

I wanted you to see me as a person who had a dream and then pursued it. And I also wanted to sit on the couch with you and play on our phones.

I want you to learn the importance of being behind the scenes to make things happen, and also to be in the spotlight. I want you to work and I want you to rest. I want you to be loud and quiet and feel comfortable being whatever any occasion calls for.

I know I was impatient about my outward success when you were very young.

I know I sometimes made you feel like I wished I were doing something else.

I hope I figured out soon enough how to be present with you. How to stop what I was doing when you needed to talk about something. How to give you my undivided attention.

I know I never wanted to play dolls with you in the bathtub.

Make-believe and pretend are not my jam. A block even.

I can't even read fiction.

Dear Naima,

The older you get, the more I love you and love hanging out with you.

I have always joked that Papa doesn't like a kid until they can deliver a book report. I admit I have the same tendencies. It's not even really a secret that I can do without most kids altogether.

I've loved you every single day of your life, but I like you more and more each day of your life. You are fun to be around.

You understand silence, and you understand humor.

Sometimes when you asked me a question and I looked confused before I could answer, it was because it takes real work for me to leave my mind.

For better or worse, sometimes I think of other people as a rude interruption of my inner world.

Even you. And I'm sorry for that.

They say you can't be friends with your kids. If being friends with you makes me a bad mom, then I'll finally admit to being a bad mom because you are most definitely my best friend. I used to say, that if I MUST spend every waking moment with another person, then I'm glad it's you.

Dear Naima,

It is so important to me to get out of your way and allow you to develop on your own. I do not want to control you. People raise their eyebrows at me for how much freedom I want you to have. So far, I have not seen you do anything destructive. You do not intentionally hurt yourself or others. You respect people. You did take a keyboard from an abandoned church building once. And sometimes we sneak into the resort pool without paying, so I wonder what rules you will bend, and I hope you get away with them when I'm not around, but I guess we'll see. How do you raise a person with enough rules to keep them safe but also teach them that authority is a bullshit concept? How do you teach the instinct not to take what isn't yours, except sometimes? How do I be the white mom of a Black girl or woman? Am I teaching you to move through the world with my privilege, and might you not be safe when I'm not around?

I hate school and I say fuck the police. How does that translate to you? We sit down for the pledge of allegiance and kneel for the national anthem. We roll our eyes at American flags and celebrations of "independence". We try to help you internalize the feeling of not trusting this country with our very lives, but also try not to scare you. You don't know about school shootings yet. You don't know that I stopped watching the news altogether after Uvalde. You know I hate intruder drills and get scared and sad for you when you've had them. I even took you out of school the day I knew about one in 1st grade.

When do I tell you that white supremacists and militia surround our home up north? On the same river where we go swimming and tap the banks with big sticks to bring out frogs.

How do I balance wonder and fear?

I don't want you to know that fear. But, I also want you to know never to be alone with a boy. Like never. I don't want to define the word, "rape" for you. I don't want to have to explain why you are not safe wearing certain shorts in the summer. I want you to be so careful when the time comes, and DO NOT GET PREGNANT before you want to. I want you to understand how important that is. How it's not even about the decision to have an abortion or not anymore. It's about legality, availability, and safety. I will take you to get an abortion if you ever want one. I will drive you to whatever state we need to go to. I hope you are so disinterested in boys and sex that it won't even be an issue. But, I've known since you were five that you are a hot tamale. And I know that everyone, and I mean everyone, will be in love with you. You had five boyfriends in kindergarten. They fought over who got to sit by you at birthday parties. They threw fists. Moms would ask what I was going to do with you. I never had the guts to ask them the same question about their sons. You didn't mind the attention. You had them all at your fingertips. But, then it was too much. They took it too far. Did it stick for you that they almost always do? You need to be hyper-aware of that. I will never forget the morning I was doing your hair and you started to cry. You said, "I don't want the boys to talk about my butt anymore." Did I turn red? Did I combust? We learned that day that Mommy leaps into immediate action and anyone who doesn't like it can go climb a tree.

Dear Naima,

You are so talented. I know you feel frustrated with how big the inside of you feels and how badly it wants to show itself to the world. I have felt this way my whole life. This is why we sing.

Dear Naima,

Will you please choose a color of the rainbow for my morning tea? Will you please always be a reflection of what about myself I need to tend to to be a better mother to you?

Dear Naima,

I love you more than anything in the world. More than the cats. You came from me. There is no other connection more intimate or meaningful than a mother and her child. You have full access to me and I can't fathom a time in my life when I would decide otherwise. What more can I do but give you everything you need? Thank you for choosing my body to house a second heartbeat for those mystical months.

I will never apologize for giving you everything I have to give. May the unwaveringness of my love and support give you the security to walk through the world knowing and seeing clearly your next steps.

If I have it, it is for you.

Love, mom

Rachel Richardson

What interests me are the nuances and subtleties of human relationships. I stage photographs that depict the ways in which individuals interact. What captures my attention are moments of pausing, what happens in-between action and conversation, because of either contemplation or overlapping of events. I investigate connections between the architectural environment and the people who inhabit it. I look at ways in which space has its effect on the individual, how it reflects the mood and atmosphere for who people are and who they want to be.

Dorthe Alstrup

Page 93: *Max*, C-Print, 30" x 40", 2001

Page 94-95: *Marcy and Desmond*, C-Print, 30" x 40", 2007

Page 96-97: *JP-Rail #2*, C-Print, 30" x 40", 2001

Boy in the window: A Parenthood in Two Parts

I.

There comes a time around twenty-two, twenty-three years old. A time when they are slightly less concerned with getting older and slightly more concerned with growing up. Less being independent and more being less of a dependent. This window is your opportunity to parent again, after being largely sidelined for your perpetual cringeworthiness the entirety of their collegiate career. Should you be so lucky, as I was, I implore you to not take this window, this responsibility lightly. There will be an entire generation of coworkers that will be eternally grateful for your engagement and participation. No trophy. Your reward is that you get to rest assured in knowing that you had nothing to do with raising the child that went off to one day become "that guy" at work.

Everybody knows who "that guy" is in the workplace. Everybody has a "that guy" at their place of work. But this was my chance, my chance to make sure our guy doesn't become that guy.

Now to be fair, my eldest son is already one of the most genuine and kind human beings I get the pleasure of being around on a regular basis. In fact, he is intellectually and emotionally gifted. So the probability of him becoming "that guy" at work is already prohibitively low. However, I take my responsibility as serious as an annual company retreat when he says that he is anxious about leaving the food service job that carried him through college to start his first forty-hour a week, nine to five. He had those first date fears in his eyes, like he really really does not want to mess this up. And I said something to the effect of "keep that same energy, you're going to need a lot of it."

I said it's alright to be scared. If you are not scared you are not trying hard enough. There's a difference between being afraid of failure and not wanting to let other people down. If you err, err on the latter. Matter of fact, if you err, err up the ladder. Sometimes it takes a couple wrongs, before we get it right. But you'll be alright. Just don't pretend you know something when you don't know something. Don't be afraid to ask for help. And when you eventually get to the point that you don't need anymore help, don't you ever forget your responsibility to those that helped you. Remember that work is a very big part of your life, but it is not your life. Remember that all of the people that we are temporarily inextricably bound to at work, have people, places and things that they are permanently bound to outside of work. Things that they love outside of work, where they actually live the rest of their lives. And here you are, son, at the very beginning of the rest of your working life.

We talked about missing old friends, making new friends and the fear of not making any friends. We talked about age gaps, ageism and the daily drip of lost youth.

We talked about the open secret of workplace culture in America.

For the most part, we are there because we are paid to be there. Using the proceeds to buy and bide our time until we are lucky enough to arrive at what we love doing or retirement. Either way, it is upon that arrival that we'll never work another day of our lives. In the meantime, these jobs that we hold along the way bind us to one another for an indeterminate amount of time. Forty hours at a time. And if we have got to be here anyway, how we pass this time is up to us until it's up. Try to be the reason that somebody at work likes to come to work. At the very least, try not to be one of the reasons someone else hates this place. Remember, it's never all your fault, but when it is, say sorry. Say thank you, as frequently as possible, for this very same reason. Because, odds are, whether we give a damn or don't give a damn we all still have to be here tomorrow. The quality of time served is, indeed, what we make it.

We talked about jobs we held, jobs we lost and jobs that wouldn't even give us the time of day.

Our dream jobs, our nightmare jobs, and the ones that got away.

We talked about how one finds their way, how one makes their way, and how one runs away.

And in the end, a career is nothing more than a mixtape of first and last days of work. The millions of buttons pushed, by you and others. From the infrequent recognition to all the coworkers who knowingly pushed your buttons. You will be surprised at the places you will be willing to move for the right gig. The job you never expect to be a "good fit," that becomes the right fit. The schooling you will be willing to suffer through just to get that next position. The coworkers you will inevitably date. And if you're lucky, like me and your mother, one might even become your mate. Admittedly, the odds are great. But that doesn't mean it isn't still fate. In fact, one of these jobs could even be the place where you take your child to work one day. However, that day is not today. Today is for remembering that you are wanted. Your services are both requested and required. Jobs are not easy to get. And so long as you treat it as such, you'll be just fine.

We talked for almost two hours, my son and I. A two hour window of time where he reminded me of all the memorable conversations I shared with all the memorable people I worked with over the years. All the jobs I had. Short and long. Good and bad. The fears that fade and the fears that remain. He reminded me of the many versions of me along the way.

Alas, should you one day find yourself the proud parent of a "that guy" at work, know we forgive you. At the very least, you can find solace in knowing that he'll always be your "that guy." Whether you missed your window or you read him this. Either way, you taught him everything you know and everything he knows.

II.

I can't believe you are almost eighteen. By the time the ink dries on this page, you will be. There are so many things I wanted you to know by now. And I can't help but feel like I am running out of time. I saw somewhere that seventy-five percent of the time we get to spend with our children is complete by the time they are twelve years old. Ninety percent by the time they are nineteen. All that to say, I miss you already. But in some ways, I feel like I know you better and better with each passing year. Perhaps that is because you are becoming more and more like me, which is not necessarily a good thing. Or maybe I am becoming more and more like you, which would be a really really good thing.

I want you to know that I look up to you, son. Not because you are 6' 5". But because you've managed to keep your nose clean and keep your books in order without the same kind of "attention to detail" oriented parenting that your grandparents provided me. As a single father for the majority of your early childhood, the best that I could do was far less "Marine" than Pop Pop and far less "Boogie Down Bronx" than MyCar. There was a lot less church and a lot more soccer. There was a new home address every other year. There were far more "bring a child to work" outings in rooms full of grown ups than playdates and sleepovers with kids your age.

I want you to know that what I couldn't offer in situational stability at times, I tried to offer in consistency of presence in the long run. And for all the better choices I could have made during those times, I will never apologize for my chronic overcompensation of loving you. Your grandfather was not easy with the compliments when I was your age. During those late teen years where the diameter of my chest was finally beginning to swell and approach the already precarious width of my head. You are such a less difficult "almost eighteen" than I was. But as Dad's mind began to turn on him and his memory began evaporating, he would consistently compliment me on how adaptable you were as a toddler in different environments. How needy you weren't. How well you followed directions. How easily you entertained yourself. How unafraid you were of grown ups. How you had a habit of treating those older than you with respect. How you made eye contact and spoke loud enough so that people his age—not too much older than I am now—could easily hear you.

I want you to know that he still hears you. That when he was complimenting me, he was complimenting you. And even though he is not around to compliment you today, he'd be quite proud of the man you have become. Despite all my unintended efforts to the contrary. I want you to know he's there, smiling that Pop Pop smile, every time you say your prayers before a game, a meal, or bedtime. I want you to know that he had a wicked jump shot. One of the purest, free-est floating shots I have ever seen. He shot jumpers like he parented, effortlessly. Change direction, stop on a dime, and let it fly. All net and celebration and trash talk, even when he was afraid it wasn't going to go in. You should've seen it. Especially, now that you are a Varsity high school hooper. Maybe you'll inherit his gift for hoops and Hail Marys. I know I didn't.

I want you to know that all the times I called your school or met with your teachers, I was not mad at you. I was afraid for you. I want you to know that I went to the Carlease Bellamy School of "F" Around and Find Out, and I was a straight "A" student. The same energy I had with you after said parent-teacher confab, I also had with your adult teacher during said parent-teacher confab. In short, she did not play. Meaning she was not about playing any games with them nor me. I learned from her that it is nice when parents have a congenial relationship with those that teach their child, however some of us have too much riding on the rearing of young Black men to leave it up to chance. Especially when every game of chance involving the probability of Black male success or survival has people that look like you and me starting with underwater odds.

I want you to know that I don't know any other way to parent. That I am grateful for my wife, your stepmother, for being a model of different and healthier ways to do so. I want you to know that I am thankful to your mother, for giving me the space to parent you the best way I know how. I want you to know that, of all the things that I can impart upon you with regards to operating as a Black man in this world, I cannot walk in your skin as a mixed-race human being. I don't know what it's like to feel partially orphaned from the pigmentation of your grandparents. I don't know what it is like for you to hear jokes about white folk from your Black friends. I don't know what it is like for you to hear racial slurs come out of the mouths of your white friends when you all gather in someone's parked car to sing-along with your favorite rap artists. I don't know if it matters to you at all. And frankly, I'm too old to know if it should. But I know that there are enough people of varying lived experiences that love what you are made of. Enough people to provide a rainbow of wisdom and a prism of love. People who want you to be yourself, because yourself is enough.

I want you to know that I am proud of the kind and compassionate man that you are becoming. The kind of man that both laughs and cries with ease. The kind of man that routinely finds beauty in the world and in other people. The kind of man that occasionally makes beauty too. You are every bit the greatness that your grandparents and uncles poured into you, and then some. And even though you and I will spend less time together in the coming years as, you put miles on your car and God puts wings on your life, I want you to know that even though time is finite it is also somehow as long or as short as we make it. That's the nature of time travel. Eighteen can become eighty-one in the blink of an eye. But what I really want you to know is, regardless of how much time we have left, I am looking forward to it. Looking forward and upward to you, and all the things I still want you to know.

Happy Birthday, Son.

Hakim Bellamy

Stepson, I have been writing to you in my head since we met, when you were three; now you are twenty, so I am writing 100 words at a time, because I don't know how else to contain our shared story (this is the title, so it's only 50 words)

As a boy, you built homes for baby snails, filled a clear plastic bowl with dirt and leaves, cottonwood sticks, and lettuce. Snails like lettuce, right? You are earth, caregiver, rock. You are adobe brick, holding warmth in winter. Someday you will be a home. You are not Tlazoltéotl, that goddess the Mexica believed ate humanity's filth, swallowing what isn't yours. It has churned in your gut, erupting as raised bumps on the tender skin behind your knees and under your arms. You scratch and scratch. Bodies try to tell us things. What is yours saying? How do we heal?

We drive near your mother's house. Can we stop and say hi? I say, Let's call her, so we don't surprise her. We wait at the stoplight. Green. Ring, ring. One block, then two, then megachurches and strip malls away from the house where you live when you are not with us. She doesn't answer. Hi, Mama… And then, Can we stop anyway? I am holding the steering wheel. I am holding your heart, remembering that morning years ago. She drove you to your dad, told him to keep you. She took it back eventually. She always takes it back.

Some years your birthday falls on Thanksgiving. There is the year we drop you and your sister off too early at your mom's, and the boyfriend you don't like is still there. There is the year she doesn't call you because you got the Covid vaccine behind her back. There is the year she says she'll make cupcakes for your class and says no because you want GMOs. I make them. I am late to a retreat so I can make them. You are sweet. You are happy and grateful. It costs me something. I won't make the cupcakes again.

The day before your sister slipped through your hands, she was in and out of the house, rubber ball bouncing from kitchen to car to backyard to bedroom. Her friend who worked the smoke and lingerie shop told her to fill a box. Bong, thong, lace gloves, pipe, boa, bustier. Your dad said, I love her energy today. The week before she was winter. Bed. iPad, SnapChat, Kardashians, lights low, curtains drawn. Out of bed means not depressed, means she's trying. Out of bed does not mean health. We don't know what's coming. But when it happens, we're not surprised.

At our former house, the house where I first met you, a toad winters deep in the soil of the sunflower bed, beneath the main bedroom window. We never see him digging, tucking in. Come spring, forgetting the toad, I turn over hard-packed dirt. He wakes, startling me, before the shovel reaches him. His presence is a sign of good soil. The weeks and months after your sister slips through your hands, I want to burrow, wait out this season, surface again in warm light. I want you to join me. Here it is quiet. Here we will be safe.

The day your sister slipped through your hands, your dad and I left to follow the ambulance. To check her in. To be with her when she woke. All six feet of you stood in the doorway of your room, not filling the space. Her bedroom floor imprinted with her seizing. The bathroom you shared covered with her sobs. You didn't ask us to stay. You didn't ask to come. We hugged you. You said your girlfriend was on her way. She bought you lunch. You stood in sunlight. You looked so small. We left you. I am so sorry.

That night, your dad got a fire going. We sat together in the living room and talked. You asked what would be different after this. Consequences? Accountability? We slept hard that night, knowing where she was, knowing she was safe. You told us you'd tried to wake us the night before. You couldn't sleep. She screamed into her phone. She slammed doors. All muted by the adobe walls of our house, by the courtyard between your side of the house and ours. You crossed the dark courtyard. Our lights off. You didn't want to wake us. What if it's nothing?

You crossed the dark courtyard at three AM as your sister raged in her room and your shared hall and bathroom. You stood outside our sliding glass doors. You tapped. We didn't hear you, didn't sense you. I always thought I would feel you if ever you really needed us, even though I didn't birth you, even though you are not mine. You tried to wake us without waking us. You crossed back to your room. Your sister's light was on, but she was quiet. You slept. Bang on our door if you have to, I said. Always wake us.

You were not made to hold her up. None of us was. She called, Dad, her voice weak, sand in her throat. Dad chopped wood in the backyard, beyond her voice. She called your name. She cried, Help me. I followed you from the kitchen to her bedroom. You stood in her doorway. You reached out to her. She fell. You couldn't hold her. None of us could. You were eighteen and five and seven and twelve all at the same time. I stepped around you. Get Dad. She seized. Call 9-1-1. You did everything right. She is still here.

She is still here. And so are you. She works with horses. She hasn't had a drink in five months. She is finding her way. She asks for and accepts help. When a family member is ill, the entire family wraps itself around that illness, becomes the channel through which we flow, narrowing in drought, whirl pooling, bashing us against rocks anchored in place over millennia. You matter. You are easy. And you don't have to be. We can bear the beautiful weight of your full humanity. Take up space. Mess up. Bang on our door. We will always answer.

Michelle Otero

Letter to Zeta

My beloved Zeta,

I keep saying to people that I still can't believe you're really gone, but it's like you're in witness protection. You are out there somewhere in the world but I will never get to see, talk to, or hold you ever again. The thought and the reality are unbearable, but it's also true. Your Zetaness is still a part of the universe that I now can only contact through love, memory, and sharing with surviving family and friends.

Even after you were no longer living at home I loved how we would hang out every week at least once, more if we were going to a drag, burlesque, wrestling, or comedy show or seeing other family. You made it a priority that we would always have one on one time. We would order takeout, and you would tell me all about your work and what you learned in school, sing me your new favorite song on Spotify, or show me a K-Pop video. You would say, "can I tell you something" or "can I ask you something" and I would answer, "always." There was nothing I loved more than being in communion with you and there was nothing off limits. When we were done catching up we'd watch *The Bachelorette* (drink water for "toxic," "drama," or "the one"), *Top Chef, Suits, Poker Face, Extraordinary Attorney Woo,* or *Heartstopper*. We'd always end with a hug and sharing "I love you." I'm grateful that is the last thing we said to each other in person.

The day afterwards I usually wouldn't talk to you. Since we would most often hang out on Tuesday nights, to trick myself into getting through your absence now, I pretend today is a Wednesday. You're busy with class and then Dungeons and Dragons with Audrey, Liv, and Claire. I was glad you had such a loving partner and friend group. I could make it through Wednesdays knowing you were thriving in other parts of your life. But now I have the rest of my lifetime of Wednesdays, where your thriving with the God you love is something I can't picture and can only hope for.

My faith has been shaken by the capriciousness and brutality of your passing. I used to have conviction. I believed everything exists, all at once, so our being remains simply where our limited perception of space, time, and identity can't perceive it. But I was also convinced I would be able to continue to watch you grow into an adult pursuing the research into Dissociative Identity Disorder you were passionate about. I looked forward to loving the adolescents you were dedicated to fostering. In a life that is limited by illness and disability, you were the center of my world and my ambitions were all in witnessing your successes.

But my witnessing for you has always included pain as well. I nursed you for two and a half years to give you a feeling of safety in a sometimes violent home. And through your early teen years, if you had to see your other mom you would ask to sleep with me when you got back. I simultaneously grieved the reason for the need and was happy to be able to soothe you and give you that safety. The music I played during the slideshow at the end of your memorial service is what we would go to sleep to: Barber's *Adagio for Strings* and Debussy's *Claire de Lune*—although at other points in your life you were partial to the soundtrack from *Music & Lyrics*, and *Maps* by the Yeah Yeah Yeahs.

The years we lived in Bethesda when you were three through second grade,were some of our happiest as we were away from your other mom and I was thriving at work. You started dance there on Saturdays which we would follow up with shopping at the Montgomery Farm Women's Cooperative Market, which sold produce, local farm raised and butchered meat, baked goods, plants, semi-precious stones, and art. But our favorite routine was on Sundays when we would walk a couple of blocks to Bethesda Bagels, then a few doors down to the local coffee roaster Quartermaine's, and finally finish in the kids section at Barnes and Noble bookstore. By three you were sight reading, starting with *Go Dog Go*. (Do you like my hat? No, I do not like your hat.)

Because your birthday was in October and the cutoff for entry to kindergarten was September 1st, I had to apply for a special exemption to get you in the year you turned five. You had to take a placement test, and I was shocked when the results came back that you had failed the fine motor skills, as you were accomplished for your age at both writing and drawing. The board told me that you had failed to copy a picture satisfactorily. So I asked you about it. "Do you remember having to copy a picture the day we went to the school?" "Yeah, but it was boring so I made it better." I shared this in my appeal letter along with pointing out that next year they would have a four foot tall fully literate kindergartener if they didn't let you in now, and no one would be happy. They acquiesced.

You were always big for your age so fit in with your older classmates although the youngest. It was sometimes hard in your younger years to get your teachers to remember though that you weren't immature, but age appropriate. Still you had an incisive intelligence that I cherished from a young age. When you were five you were complaining that I wouldn't cross the street with you against the light. I explained about the categorical imperative, which says if it's not moral for everyone to do it it's not moral for you to do it. One day we were on the metro. As always you had me read all the signs in the train car to you, so you were well aware of the rules. When two teenage girls jumped through the closing doors you observed with concern, "Mommy, that's not the categor pertive!"

Still you were innocent and guileless. One morning you ran into my bedroom wide eyed and said, “Don’t come into the living room!” Of course I did and found an explosion of craft supplies including an impressive amount of glitter. Not all surprises were bad though: another morning you came in, all dressed up, with a paper for my boyfriend Kirpal and me saying, “You are invited to Swan Lake with only the swan” which you performed with gusto to your favorite VHS tape.

You also had a creative sense of humor. You came up with the following jokes at age three:

Knock knock
Who’s there?
Everybody
Everybody who?
Everybody in the whole wide world coming to your house in a police car for a party!

But my absolutely favorite was:

Knock knock
Who’s there?
Tree
Tree who?
Ha ha! No tree!

It is worthy of a Zen koan.

Seeing how much it cracked me up you told it over and over. You never cared about fitting in and didn’t understand why other children sometimes found you odd. You did, after all, eat worms. When you found yourself being bullied in the second grade along with some younger kids, you organized them into a defensive phalanx so that the next time Michael approached you were able to grab him by the arm and helicopter him around until you sent him flying. The playground attendants were either as oblivious as they had been to the bullying or figured as I did that he had it coming and it was you who reported this to me matter of factly when I asked about your day. I did find it a little awkward as a parenting moment while I was taking you to Quaker meetings on the weekend, but mostly I was proud of your resilience and told you so.

I wish you hadn’t needed your resilience so much, between the abuse, mental health, and physical disabilities you suffered and dealing with mine as well. When we moved back to Boston the summer before third grade I knew you would need support due to being exposed again to your other mom, so I put you in therapy.

Still the support couldn't overcome the emotional chaos of your other household, and what I later found out was abuse. You started having anxiety attacks at nine and I started my court fight to limit your exposure to your other parent, hampered by the fact that your therapist refused to get involved. At twelve you started to self-harm, and at fourteen you were hospitalized for suicidality for the first time. You had both Complex Post-Traumatic Stress Disorder and Dissociative Identity Disorder (DID). You were very active in your own mental health treatment journey, finding particular help in Dialectical Behavioral Therapy. Its creator, Marsha Linnehan, was your hero and you soon gave up your focus on sociolinguistics (where you had wanted to study how other languages deal with non-binary and other gender identities) and set your aim on doing for DID what Linnehan did for borderline personality disorder.

Despite spending the majority of your senior year in treatment, you graduated Cambridge Rindge and Latin School with glowing recommendations from your teachers. Due to my own hospitalization following your first suicide attempt in December of your senior year, you joined DCF custody and chose to remain a part of its voluntary adult placement program after you turned eighteen, taking advantage of their many supportive resources while still remaining independent. I am so proud of you that despite still suffering from relapses with your chronic suicidality you managed to graduate with an associates in psychology from Massasoit Community College and transferred to UMass Boston, where you were hired as a research assistant in an LGBTQ+ lab. You were planning on presenting a poster at the American Psychological Association this summer and were talking about getting engaged in the spring. But I have learned that chronic suicidality doesn't care about daily happiness and all it took was a bad day.

As difficult as parts of your life and its ending were, you were also a vibrant student who knew four writing systems by age twelve, a talented dancer, artist, and musician, a devoted friend, spawn, and partner, and a passionate activist. Before you had become what you had recently called "a baby Marxist," at age thirteen I was upset when I caught you playing Billionaire Tycoon on your phone. "But Mommy," you said with a twinkle in your eye, "I'm creating jobs!" I sent you to your room. Then there was the time where you burnt down a village in *Minecraft* and I made you build a Red Cross center. By high school though you were writing anti-capitalist screeds for the school newspaper, and by the end of your life I would be admiring you for your dedicated abolitionist and anti-genocidal activism.

Sometimes it was hard not to annoy you with my pride. One day in early high school I let out a joyful sound that you were listening to *Rebel Rebel* by David Bowie, and you objected, "Mom, you're ruining it!" Still you enjoyed the ways we were connected, and we associated ourselves with Lorelei and Rory on the *Gilmore*

Girls, a deeply devoted single mom and kid against the world. You called me Birth Giver. I called you Loin Fruit, and later when you were too old for the non-binary word kid, my spawn.

You made me a better person, and more myself, as you always unquestioningly supported my identities, including being non-binary, and welcomed me under the trans umbrella where cis has never fit. Now, as I try to find my way forward I think about every choice, "would you be proud of me or happy for me?" I am dedicated to trying to care for myself with the parental love I gave you. I don't understand a future without you but I am grateful to be rooted to the here and now, one breath at a time, by all my loving family, friends, and community. I was moved at your memorial by all that people shared, as every bit of you from another corner of your life is a gift that I cherish.

Thank you for giving me the greatest gift of all: the privilege of being your mom. I struggled with that word after you died. Widows and orphans have words that explain their loss immediately to others. I found the Hebrew word Shakula for a mother that has lost a child, literally "a reversal of the natural order." It is now a name I carry everywhere as I cannot bear to have people know me without knowing this most important part of me—that I am a survivor of a lost world, forever estranged from my home, the love of my life.

Still I am and will always be a mother, even now that you are gone, as I now nurture your memory as I once did you, and honor it by striving to live by your ideals and hopes for me and our community. Trying to parent myself is hard when I struggle to even brush my teeth in a world without you. Without a job, a partner, or school, the future without you stretches on in unbearable emptiness. All I can do is fill my present moment by moment. I am so lucky to have my own mom five blocks away and relish her company and care. I go to shows, basking in community even when I am alone, sometimes with your partner Audrey, whose presence at our family holidays makes the ache of your absence less. I struggle with moments where I anticipate your laughter or fervent discussion, and my shoulder feels empty where you would lay your head. Your cousins have been great, inviting me out to the movies and coming to watch shows with me where you would have been, especially Word Prom, our Oscars—the Scripps National Spelling Bee finals. This year we replaced water with Mike's Hard Lemonade. (Drink for eponyms, toponyms, Sanskrit, Arabic, or Persian!) But sharing the moment with your generation still isn't being in shared communion with you.

I miss your vibrant energy that you brought to everything you explored and created. I am carefully crafting meaning where watching and helping to guide your growth were everything I hoped to accomplish in this world. Now I am returning to my words in the hope that diction and syntax can build a scaffolding to guide me through my endless days. I write to you to feel the fullness of our life together enveloping me. I don't know if I'll ever stop having nights where I keen for you and am haunted by imaginings of your final moments, begging for sleep to allow me to see you in dreams. Thank you for those visitations and for blessing me with the grace in your felt presence, which I cling to upon waking.

This weekend I buried your ashes in a grave that waits for me to join you, and beneath the Japanese maple tree you wanted to become. Watching it grow in the coming years, its leaves turning the red of your colored hair, will give me peace in seeing you live on in the physical world. You were born of my body and I carry the scar of your birth as a sacred connection, bookmarking your life. I love and live for you forever, Loin Fruit.

Mommy

Deborah Haber

My work focuses on subjects close to home and to my life—friends, family, my gardens, place and my community. The notion of relationships, whether with people or place is paramount. Motherhood gave me a new, intimate subject close at hand and I dove into photographing my son early on. In the long photographic tradition of portraits, and family photos, from Julia Margaret Cameron, to August Sander, to Diane Arbus, to Judith Black, to Sally Mann and so many others, I strove to tease out the moments, the friendships, the fun and the quiet of my son growing up. None of the work was staged, and all of it allowed me an opportunity to be present in the moments of our life. In my work making cyanotypes I continued (and continue) to incorporate family negatives from the very personal to ancestors (usually unknown to me) in my work. The images included in this book are from the mid-1990's. As my work has evolved, the long line of the generations continues to have a sustaining power for my heart and the narratives I create.

Cynthia Katz

Right: *Dylan Looking Blue*, cyanotype, 1995

Page 120-121: *Bath*, silver gelatin print, 1995

Page 122-123: *Sprinkler*, silver gelatin print, 1994

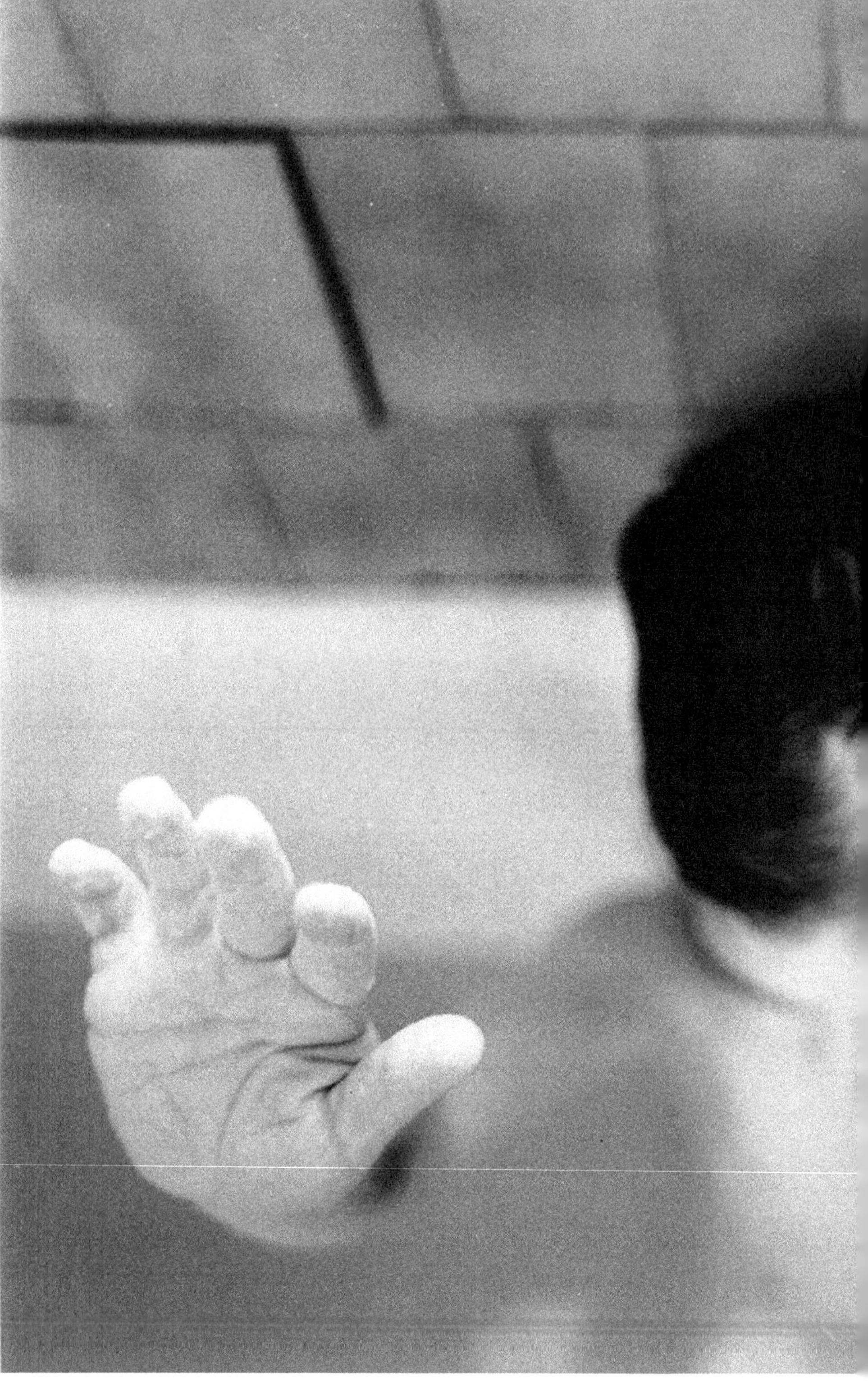

Dear Reader,

For the longest time I didn't want children. I thought that to be a parent was to sacrifice your *self*, in every sense of the word. It wasn't until I was in my 20's, visiting my high school photography teacher and mentor, and saw how she interacted with her son that I realized parenting could be more things than what the mythology about motherhood allowed.

Her son was maybe three, or four, or five, and drew me a picture. But after a short while he started to get upset, I think because we were no longer paying attention to him. My mentor and eventually friend calmly asked him, "are you hungry? Are you sad?" and with a few simple questions disarmed his tantrum and helped him identify his emotions. And then we went back to our conversation. It was magical. (At least, it was in my memory.)

Decades later I visited her with my own son, who was three, or four, or five. We went for a walk in a nearby park, and after a while Oscar fell further and further behind. Not because we were walking quickly, but because he felt ignored. I asked if he was hungry, or sad, or tired. He replied yes, and we kept walking, back to her house and to a snack.

What I've learned through this whole parenting journey is that my goal as a parent is to help my kid become a kind, self-aware person, and that everything else is gravy. I've learned to just be.

Because to be honest, parenting today is rough.

In 2024, the US Surgeon General Vivek Murthy warned that parents' stress levels were a public health crisis, as forty-eight percent of parents reported that most days the stress was overwhelming, compared to twenty-six percent of other adults (Office of the US Surgeon General, 2024, p. 9). While this may have told us that we were not alone in the struggle, it also painted a bleak picture.

Parenting takes more time and resources than it did a generation ago. Rising economic insecurities and inequalities, along with the intense pressure to spend more time and resources on children, have left parents isolated and depressed (Nomaguchi & Milkie, 2020). It's made worse in the US where parenting is seen as an individual activity and responsibility. There are few federally mandated supports for parents—no paid family leave, no universal child care, and certainly no sense of parenting as a shared or communal responsibility or as a form of work as important as an out-of-home job.

Children have more challenges as well. The Centers for Disease Control released data in 2024 that showed a rise in depression among youth, with fifty-three percent of female-identified students reported persistent feelings of persistent sadness, almost double from ten years before, and twenty-eight percent of male-identifying students. More than twice the number of LGBTQ+ youth than straight students reported persistent sadness or hopelessness, and twenty percent of LGBTQ+ youth reported suicidal feelings. It's beyond time to shout from the rooftops and sound the alarm.

As I write this, Presidential Executive Orders, legislation and Supreme Court decisions have shown how little parents are valued. College loans have been capped, birthright citizenship challenged, and for my family, any mention of us in books or media can be purged as something dangerous, poisonous or contagious.

I'm married to another woman, and we're raising a son in the conservative state of Ohio. When our son was born, my wife wasn't listed on his birth certificate and she had no parental rights (even though, as she likes to remind him a lot, she caught him during birth). On July 27, 2015, the three of us marched down to our rural county courthouse to get married—well, my wife and I got married while our four year old looked bored, only holding on with the bribe of ice cream. By then we'd been together for almost fifteen years, but with the marriage certificate she could adopt him.

I worry about him being bullied. I worry about other parents or teachers making him uncomfortable. I worry if he's ever going to feel ashamed of our family.

But it turns out I don't have to worry so much about him, after all. He cares about the world and the creatures in it. He's wicked smart. He has an acerbic wit. He does his chores with minimal grumbling. He cares deeply for his friends' emotional well-being. He can raise one eyebrow independently of the other, and he flosses regularly.

One day when I picked him up from pre-school, a girl asked him who was his "real mom."

He looked at her, eyes narrowed even at three, or four, or five years old, and shouted, "I have **two** moms!"

This confidence has played out time and again in his young life. Whenever he has been confronted about our family, however benignly, this has basically been his response—a statement of fact with a little defiance thrown in. He has a tight group of friends and it's not a thing that we are his parents. I have to have faith that his friends will have his back when he is confronted about our family, and that he will have theirs when they are unjustly challenged by the world.

Parenting is one of the hardest things I've ever done, but also the most joyful. We laugh together often. Ultimately, parenting is a constant gesture towards hope and optimism. Even though I am super pissed off about the state of our country, and what it means for our son's future, I know I have to place my faith in him and his peers, and believe they will do better.

Reader, I hope you've found that hope in these pages. You've been given a glimpse of other parents' journeys, in both text and image, and hopefully have seen yourself and possibilities within these pages. Even as the world turns to shit, there's still hope.

Lee Fearnside
August, 2025

About the Editors

Robin Stock is a career fundraiser, communicator and strategist. By day, she raises money to support research, access and equity in the higher education sector. Her side hustle as a ghostwriter of romance novels has allowed her to see more than two-dozen of her stories in international publication. She is an avid rock hunter, voracious reader, lover of music, sports and food. She lives in Perrysburg, Ohio with her husband Jesse, with whom she shares two adult children, Alia and London.

Lee Fearnside is an artist, photographer, editor and curator. Her work has always been about social positioning in our world, whether the topic is scars of the body, aniamls adapting to human behavior, or editing anthologies. She recently published *Death Never Dies: Mourning 2020 through the Lives and Deaths of Public Figures*, which won the Gold Medal in Pop Culture from the Independent Publishers Book Awards and the silver medal in Non-Fiction Anthologies from the Midwest Book Awards. She lives in Toledo, Ohio, with her wife, son, and two dogs.

About the Contributors

Dorthe Alstrup was born and raised in Denmark. She earned a BA in advertising and editorial photography from Kent Institute of Art and Design in England and an MFA in photography from the Rhode Island School of Design, US. She has been an Artist in Residence at the Banff Centre for the Arts in Canada and participated in the Artist in the Marketplace program at the Bronx Museum of the Arts, New York. Dorthe has received a number of grants, including from: Rhode Island State Council for the Arts (RI), the American-Scandinavian foundation (Denmark),tThe Danish Contemporary Art Foundation (Denmark), and the Barbara Spohr Award (Canada). She won First Price in Center's 2008 Singular Image Awards in the color category. Dorthe has exhibited work in Australia, Denmark, Canada, England, Japan, and the U.S, including the Bronx Museum of the Arts (NY), Photographic Center Northwest (WA), the Griffin Museum of Photography (MA), and Jen Bekman Gallery (NY). Dorthe now lives and works in Denmark.

Hakim Bellamy is the Inaugural Poet Laureate of Albuquerque (2012-2014), a two-time National Poetry Slam Champion (2005-2006) and past Creative Writing Chair at New Mexico School for the Arts. His poetry has been published on the Albuquerque Convention Center, on the outside of a library, in inner-city buses, and in numerous anthologies across the globe. Bellamy was recognized as an honorable mention for the University of New Mexico Paul Bartlett Ré Peace Prize for his work as a community organizer and journalist in 2007 and later awarded the Career Achievement Award for the same Prize in 2018. In 2017 he was named a Kennedy Center Citizen Artist Fellow and previously served as the on-air television host for New Mexico PBS's *¡COLORES!* program for three years. Prior to earning a law degree at the University of New Mexico School of Law, Bellamy served as deputy director for the City of Albuquerque Department of Arts and Culture from 2018 to 2022.

Caitlin Cacciatore (she/her/hers) is a poet and essayist based on the outskirts of New York City. Caitlin believes that literature has the power to change minds and start movements, and considers herself a "poet of testimony." Caitlin's poetry has appeared in over a dozen literary magazines, journals, and anthologies, including B*acopa Literary Review*, *Sunlight Press*, and *The Good Life Review*. Caitlin was long-listed for the international erbacce-prize in 2021, 2022, and 2023. Her poem *Still Life with Roses* was nominated for a 2024 'Best of the Net' anthology award. Similarly, *Memento Mori* was nominated for a Pushcart Prize. Her creative non-fiction and essays have appeared in *Rebellious Magazine for Women*, on StarTrek.com, and in the *422 Anthology*. You can find her essay on solastalgia in an upcoming anthology by Four Palaces Publishing. You can find her online at caitlincacciatore.wordpress.com.

Ally Day, PhD, is an experienced scholar in Disability Studies, Gender Studies and Sexuality Studies. Her book, *The Political Economy of Stigma: HIV, Memoir, Medicine and Crip Positionalities* (The Ohio State University Press, 2021) won the 2022 Alison Piepmeier Prize from the National Women's Studies Association. In addition, she has written nineteen peer reviewed articles and book chapters and is co-producer and lead researcher of the *HIV in the Rust Belt Film Project* (dir. Holly Hey); the episode *Sister Eileen and Her Boyz* received national distribution on PBS stations through NETA. She is also co-founder, co-producer, and co-host of the *Telling It Our Way* Podcast (WGTE Public Media), which received the 2025 American Association on Intellectual and Developmental Disabilities (AAIDD) Media Award and the Press Club of Toledo's Touchstone Journalism Award. Her forthcoming book, *Gestational Ableism: Disability, Pregnancy and the Future of Care* addresses the intersection of disability and pregnancy and includes qualitative research with disabled pregnant people about how they navigate complex and often oppressive medical systems. Dr. Day works as a Research Navigator for Maine Health following her tenure as an Associate Professor of Disability Studies at the University of Toledo. Outside of her research and writing, Dr. Day is a certified doula and accessible yoga instructor.

Curtis A. Deeter is an author of fantasy, science fiction, and horror. When he is not writing, he enjoys spending time with his family, discovering new music, and taste-testing craft beer at local breweries.

Maggie Denk-Leigh is a Professor and Division Chair for Visual Arts and Crafts at the Cleveland Institute of Art in Cleveland, Ohio. Beginning at CIA in 1999 in the Printmaking program, she has taught courses in lithography, etching, screenprint, relief and digital media, and oversees a letterpress studio for a book arts course. Denk-Leigh is a founding board member, and the current Board Vice President at the Morgan Art of Papermaking Conservatory & Educational Foundation, a hand papermaking and book arts center in Cleveland, Ohio. As a practicing artist, Denk-Leigh explores anthropological associations through printed and sculptural works. She received her BA from Xavier University in Cincinnati, Ohio and her MFA in Printmaking from Clemson University, South Carolina.

Deborah Haber is a genderqueer and bisexual writer, musician, and artist from the Greater Boston area. She attended Bryn Mawr College and is lucky to have lived with a sister, four parents, and in five countries. A spoonie zebra, disabled by Ehlers Danlos Syndrome, chronic fatigue syndrome, PTSD, and a host of other ailments, Deborah spends most of her time in bed. Throughout her life though she has pet giant clams on the Great Barrier Reef and swum with whale sharks in Mexico, recorded multiple CDs of her original songs, worked with poison control, been a national protest organizer, and performed as the drag king Phallus B Toklas. Nothing however compares to motherhood of her late child Zeta as her greatest experience.

Holly Hey is an independent filmmaker living in Ohio, teaching at the University of Toledo, and making documentary and experimental films. Her work focuses on social justice issues like queer identity, HIV history, clean water access, and criminal justice reform. Her films and videos have screened across the country and internationally, as well. Holly is a NETA (The National Educational Telecommunications Association) producer with multiple titles receiving national distribution. Her festival highlights include The Ann Arbor Film Festival, The Athens International Film Festival, The Big Muddy Film Festival, and the Queens World Film Festival. Her scholarly research focuses on work-based learning, subjective experience, and the language of the image. Holly holds a BFA in photography from Ohio University and a MFA in film from The School of the Art Institute of Chicago.

Erin Holscher Almazan is a Professor of Printmaking and Drawing at the University of Dayton in Dayton, Ohio. Erin is a native of North Dakota. She received a BFA in Fine Arts from Minnesota State University Moorhead and an MFA from Rochester Institute of Technology, in Rochester, New York. She taught as an Adjunct Instructor in Foundations at Rochester Institute of Technology prior to teaching at the University of Dayton. She has completed two printmaking residencies at the Frans Masereel Centrum in Kasterlee, Belgium. Erin's work has been exhibited nationally and internationally and has been included in exhibitions in connection with the Southern Graphics Printmaking Council and the Mid-America Print Council. Erin resides in Dayton with her husband and two sons.

Cynthia Katz is an award-winning photo-based artist working in the Boston area. Process and discovery have been guiding forces that link all her work. This work has been described as being both mysterious and familiar, has been shown regionally and nationally, most recently at Three Stones Gallery, Jessica Hagen Gallery, the Danforth Art Museum, the Fitchburg Art Museum, and Soho Photo Gallery in New York City. In 2024 Katz was recognized by LensCulture's Art Photography Awards as a finalist and a juror's pick. She was awarded the Photography Prize at the 2024 Fitchburg Art Museum's Exhibition of Art and Craft and was the first prize recipient in Soho Photo Gallery's 2024 Alternative Process Competition. Her work is published in journals, books and blogs, including Manifest's *International Photography Annual 3*, SlowSpace.org and *LensCulture*. Cynthia's recent presentations include "Handmade Photographs" at the Photographic Resource Center in Boston, Three Stones Gallery and at Concord Art. She is represented by Jessica Hagen Gallery in Newport, Rhode Island. Cynthia earned a BFA in Photography from the University of New Hampshire and an MFA in Photography from Bennington College. She maintains a studio at The Umbrella

Arts Center in Concord, Massachusetts, and she lives in West Concord.

Michael Kocinski is a poet, illustrator, and grant evaluator. He lives in Columbus, Ohio with his wife and their two sons—their daughter lives in Charlotte, NC and she will probably never return to the Midwest. Michael's poems have been published in *The Mid-American Review, Peachfuzz, Glass: A Journal of Poetry,* and others. He had his first solo art show in December of 2024. He also posted over 300 species on iNaturalist in 2024. He can be found on Instagram: @michael_kocinski; or he can be found fishing the Olentangy River watershed, birdwatching, or browsing comics at the Laughing Ogre in Clintonville.

D.S. Mohan's writings explore the need to question our beliefs on what has always been. Trying, every day, to bypass the mindless pitfalls established to sidetrack people from staying informed and grounded in what is truly important, she's focused on continuing difficult discussions. Her interests in writing extend from board books to novels and poetry for adults. A firm believer that each of us needs to speak up for our own story, because no one else will do it for us, she strives to live her life with peace, passion, and purpose.

Michelle Otero is the author of *Vessels: A Memoir of Borders*, and *Bosque: Poems,* and *Malinche's Daughter*. A former Albuquerque Poet Laureate (2018–2020), she co-edited the award-winning *22 Poems and a Prayer for El Paso* and *New Mexico Poetry Anthology 2023*. Founder of ArteSana Creative Consulting and Gozo: a creative feast for women & nonbinary writers in Oaxaca, she uses storytelling to build community and foster healing. A member of the Macondo Writers Workshop, her work has appeared, or is forthcoming, in *POETRY, American Poetry Review, Shenandoah*, and *The Best of Brevity*. Her work centers memory, justice, and cultural identity across borders and generations.

Sarah Rainey-Smithback is an Associate Professor in the School of Cultural and Critical Studies and the Women's, Gender, and Sexuality Studies Program at Bowling Green State University. Her work focuses on the intimate and reproductive lives of sexually marginalized populations (LGBT people, people with disabilities, and people of color), and has appeared in *Ms. Magazine, the Journal of Literary and Cultural Disability Studies, Hypatia, Sexualities, Lesbian and Gay Psychology Review*, and *AIDS Education and Prevention*. Her books include *Love, Sex, and Disability: The Pleasures of Care* (2011, Lynne Rienner Publishers) and *Crip Love Onscreen: Representing Love, Sex, and Disability* (The Ohio State University Press, 2026). She lives in Ohio with her husband, many children, and dogs.

Rachel Richardson is a veteran jazz and folk singer, guitarist, published author, cultural event and public art coordinator, and all-around performer. She is a lifelong community activist. As a professional advocate for victims of domestic violence, she co-founded Independent Advocates in 2007, which produced a Court Watch Report in 2011 recommending a Domestic Violence Court in Lucas County. As the founder and CEO of Rachel Richardson Productions, she has co-ordinated over 65 murals in downtown Toledo and surrounding neighborhoods. She is the Artistic Director of Jazz Alley in Toledo's Glass City Center. Rachel holds a Bachelor of Arts in Interdisciplinary Studies in Sociology, Ethnic Studies, and Non-Profit Management from the University of Toledo. Rachel and her family co-wrote and illustrated *Just Worms for Dinner* in 2020, a children's book and call to arms to collect worms for Donald Trump to eat in prison. She co-authored *On Drowning Rats: How Two Women Took Down a Sexual Harasser and How You Can, Too* with Cami Roth Szirotnyak. She was a longtime Toledo Free Press Star columnist, and has been published in several Chimera Projects anthologies including award-winning *Death Never Dies* (2021) and *Spark* (2024). She appears in *SWELL Magazine*. Rachel is a product of Toledo, Ohio.

Sandra Rivers-Gill is an award-winning poet, playwright and teaching artist. Her writing often explores themes of family and social justice. She has led poetry residencies for Naomi Inc., and Otterbein Senior Living Communities; and West Toledo and Sandusky Libraries through Creative Aging Ohio. She currently serves as the Poet Ambassador of Northwest Ohio. Her poetry has been featured in numerous journals and anthologies. Her debut poetry collection, *As We Cover Ourselves With Light*, is a finalist for the 2024 Eric Hoffer Book Award.

Janalee Stock is a retired registered nurse and community activist from Athens, Ohio. She worked as a school nurse for Athens City Schools before retiring in 2016. Since then, she has become involved in various community initiatives and non-profit work, including co-founding the Women for Recovery organization. Janalee has been honored at the local and state level for her work to support women who are recovering from addiction, and for her work in reducing the use of plastics as a youth educator for Athens ReThink Plastics. She is a mother of four, a grandmother of nine, a fitness buff and personal trainer, and a political activist who writes op-ed pieces regularly for local news sources, including the Athens County Independent.